WARRIOR

ON THE

BATTLEFIELD

MEHABOOB ISMAIL

First Published in April 2023

ISBN: 978-93-5741-672-6

BLUEROSE PUBLISHERS

www.bluerosepublishers.com

info@bluerosepublishers.com

+91 8882 898 898

Cover Design:

Yash

Typographic Design:

Tanya Raj Upadhyay

Distributed by: BlueRose, Amazon, Flipkart

Preface

I've written this book to share the lessons I've learned, in the hope that they'll provide you with some clarity and guidance to live what I call a greater life. It's up to you what you take from my stories, research and thoughts. I accept that some ideas will resonate, while others will feel uncomfortable. Nevertheless, I do believe that if you can apply the concepts I discuss within the course of this book, you'll experience incredible positive changes in your life.

I'm not a philosopher, a psychologist, a scientist or a religious leader. I'm simply someone who likes to learn and share my wisdom with others, hoping that it may release them from undesirable feelings and increase feelings of joy and motivation.

Life is a battle. You not only fight external battles with the world outside but also internal battles with your own destructive and evil qualities. The world in which you live is a **battlefield**. Your mind and body are also battlefields. It is where you fight physical and mental battles against your own evil, negative, or unlawful tendencies, qualities, desires, thoughts and attitudes. In the sacrifice of life, you serve both good and evil. Sometimes circumstances and sometimes your own desires and expectations influence your actions and decisions.

In our modern society, young people are fed information which puts pressure on them to meet needs that are often unrealistic. They are inundated with images as to how they are meant to look, what they are meant to have and how they are meant to behave, all based on the assumption that this is important to life. If young people feel that they do not meet the images that are portrayed to them via the media or peers, they can often feel different, that they are not good enough or disadvantaged which, if not dealt with appropriately, can lead to depression as well as problems with self-esteem, and confidence.

My first attempt is a message to youngsters who are broken from their dreams, and ambitions and also due to social pressures. When they fail to fix all the broken pieces, they go through failures and fail to deal with emotional pain, also which causes a lot of pressure from the climate of opinions, and then they fall into ugly depression, anxiety, and panic attacks. Later on when they fail to come out from it, eventually it drags them to a suicidal zone. They think of ending up their life to get rid of their internal pain. Isn't it? We often hear or read these kinds of news on social media.

Do you know what causes a major impact on us? It is when we lose our dear friends or any family members due to depression. It creates a major impact on our lives.

I have closely observed all of these thick and thin happening with the young generation. That's what made me write this book. Hence, I have shared some tips and ways to come out from darkness to light. This book will be your roadmap to building yourself and leading a happy life.

We all feel lost sometimes. Just because people don't seem this way on the outside, doesn't mean they don't feel these emotions inside. It's hard when you're surrounded by people your own age who all seem like they have their life together, but in reality, they are just really good at faking it. Even the people who are successful now once felt lost in life.

Even if you feel lost in life now, do not give up. Whether you had a terrible childhood or you've suffered from some difficult experiences in life, you should be thankful for it. Why? Because the struggle you are in today is developing the strength you need for tomorrow. **We are all warriors in life and we are scared from time-being issues. Trust me, no worries will last forever. You know after heavy rain-fall, of course, sunshine will come.**

It's okay to talk about the things you feel, about your depression, your anxiety and your stress and all the things you worry about, it's okay to struggle with these things in order to how to deal with it. It's okay not to know where to begin or how to deal with it or how to heal. It's all okay my friend but don't keep everything inside you. Talk about how you feel and what you feel, be honest and be open about it. It's okay to break down in tears, this is how you change, and this is how you will heal, by talking about it and by letting the people who care about you to know what it is you're holding so far. Don't bottle up inside in your heart, don't bury it and let it out and let the sunlight in. Like this your journey begins. Like this you grow properly.

It is so easy to let things worry us, way more than they should. Sometimes we are not even sure what we are worrying about. We tend to make up stories and scenarios in our head of 'what if', 'how will I?', and Could it be that...?', when in reality, we would have no visibility of what will actually happen. This is what makes us worriers.

As long as you are alive, you still have a chance.

What if we try to shift our mindset from being a worrier, to being a warrior? What if we stop worrying about what could happen, and instead use our energy to transform ourselves into warriors to be ready for whatever happens? We would then be able to put our worries aside because we would be ready for whatever life decides to throw at us.

Your mind has enormous power. Indeed, your mind is your most important performance resource. How you see and respond to the events of life and work is shaped by **your mindset and patterns of thinking**. Therefore, an essential key to success is to train your mind and use it wisely

You are the architect of your **frame of mind.** You decide how you will perceive and process life and work events. You make the decision if your mindset is positive or negative. If you want to feel better, you have to think better. In order to be positive in the way you feel, it is necessary to be disciplined in the way you think.

Just like the lotus, we too have the ability to rise from the mud, bloom out of darkness, and radiate into the world."

Famous Jewish Buddhist Goldie Hawn says this precious bloom is her favourite. She writes: "The lotus is the most beautiful flower; whose petals open one by one. But it will only grow in the mud. In order to grow and gain wisdom, first, you must have the mud — the obstacles of life and its suffering. The mud speaks of the common ground that humans share, no matter what our stations in life. Whether we have it all or we have nothing, we are all faced with the same obstacles: sadness, loss, illness, dying and death. If we are to strive as human beings to gain more wisdom, more kindness, and more compassion, we must have the intention to grow as a lotus and open each petal one by one."

it's very difficult to move forward holding the mountain on your shoulders, it's time to release the weight which is dragging you back. Say this to yourself I am learning each and every day to allow the space between where I am and where I want to be and inspire me and not terrify me.

Make a practice of asking for what you really want. No self-imposed guilt. No self-imposed shame. Do not be afraid to voice what you desire or what you really deserve. Be, Live, Enjoy.

I believe that every person on this planet is here to make a difference. I'm devoted to helping you find your purpose so you can add value to our world, which is in such turmoil. If we can collectively become conscious citizens of this planet, we'll lessen the burden we place on it. By living to your full potential, you'll not only change your world, but you'll also change the world around you, too.

This book requires you to commit to a better you right now. My aim is to help you become better than the person you were yesterday, every day, in each and every way, for the rest of your life. If you wake up with this desire in your mind and then consciously follow up on it, you'll be surprised by how much inspiration you find. Your life will begin to reflect your commitment to progress.

Mate, thank you! if you are reading this I need you to hold my hand until the last page of this book – are you ready, let's get there together.

Acknowledgements

Dear Parents,

(Mr. Ismail and Mrs. Jaibun)

I offer my sincerest gratitude to my parents. Dear Mom and Dad, you always guiding me in the right direction and putting me up without any doubt. I am always thankful to such wonderful parents in the world. No amount of words will be enough to tell how grateful I am to you. Having parents like you are the biggest of all blessings!

Dear Mom and Dad, I have let so many years pass without thanking you both. But you haven't let a single second pass without loving me unconditionally. Everything that I learned in life is from you two. You are the reason behind my successes and the inspiration behind my endeavours! Thank you so much, Mom and Dad, for understanding me so well, and for letting me choose my own dream. I always love to be your kid. I wish everyone got parents like mine – supportive, understanding, and kind! Thank you for giving me the best life possible.

Thank you so much for the inspiration and support motivation that you have given me. Without both of you, I might not be the person I am right now. You always stood by my side in every situation, always showering gentle care and love and making every moment of my life so special. Your hugs give me so many positive vibes to face any problems in my life and your love makes my world fill with many happiness.

My dear parents, you let go of your dreams and sacrificed a ton so that I can achieve mine. I cannot thank you enough in this lifetime for your contribution to my life. Love you a lot and respect from your son. Thank you for giving me such a beautiful life.

Dear Sister Fatima, I'm extremely fortunate to have such a down-to-earth and loving sister to lean on and share my thoughts with. Thank you for lending an ear when nobody else would, and for the bond we share.

Dear Mulla Family, thank you to the most incredible **family** I could ask for. I wanted to reach out and express my gratitude for all of your help. You all are the most important people in the world to me. Thanks for being my rock.

There are few major important people in my life who have shaped my life.

Dear Ashok Sir,

I express my deepest gratitude to my mentor and my beloved brother **Ashok sir,** whose teachings have been the foundation of how I live my life. My professional and personal life master has been my inspiration and example in living a life of integrity and good character.

Having the opportunity to learn from you has made a substantial change in my career. When we first began working together, I never imagined I would be able to make as much progress as I have. Thanks to you, I moved up to good progress in my professional growth.

Your training from basic to team management showed me a whole new path to improving all the operations. Before working with you, I struggled to lead and struggled with a lack of motivation. Thanks to the time we spent planning team-building best practices.

Having you as a mentor has changed my life for the better. I truly appreciate everything that you have done for me. I look forward to working with you in the future

I am blessed to have you as my mentor. Thank you for your guidance and support in all the ups and down. Being under your wing has been a blessing to my life. I loved the quality you help someone else like you have really helped me. Accept my heartfelt appreciation note. Thank you for your kindness and help. May God Bless you abundantly!

Dear Jamu,

Dearest Mate, it is weird that my wingman is not really a man but a woman. I know I still fight like a kid, and I'll continue to do so. I know that we will have different journeys in our lives, but what will always be common is our friendship that stretches way beyond our individual intertwined worlds, and I hope it will stay, come what may. Here's to being best friend.

You help me see the world from a new and fresh perspective. You help me to understand what the world is like for a female. You help me become a better friend, more sensitive, understanding, and empathetic, and all in all a way a better human being. This friendship has really helped me grow and evolve as a person, and I am so glad. I hope so we are best friends till your teeth fall off. Thanks for scolding me for my mistakes and also appreciating me little me whenever I manage to do okay things.

One special thing I love about you is that you always wear a smile even in difficult times and you face it like A warrior mate and that really inspired me and I accepted you as my inspiration too. you are one true beautiful lady. I'm really proud of you and I really appreciate whatever you do.

Thank you just for being there for me, for making me feel supported, loved, and cared for. No matter how far we may be, we'd always be close to each other's hearts. I'm thankful to you for sharing such a wonderful bonding with me.

Thanks for always cheering me up whenever life knocks me down. Thank you so much for being my boss lady! **A loads of hugs, love from your meh.**

In my life I got true friends like a family who made my life so colourful and filled with a lot of positivity, my life is incomplete without all these people

- ➢ **Girish Itagi**
- ➢ **Prasad H**
- ➢ **Santosh N M**
- ➢ **Prashant S**
- ➢ **Nelson M**
- ➢ **Harish Itagi**
- ➢ **Leyla (Neda)**

Life is beautiful because best friends like you're there. Every single word of yours inspires me and gives me new motivation. Thanks for understanding me better than me.

No doubt life has given me so many new faces and relationships. But nothing is as sweeter as our friendship. I'm so lucky to call you my buddies. Thanks for making friendship mean such a magical thing to me.

You're always there to hear me whether I was cracking a stupid joke, complaining about life or just blabbering. Thanks for being a non-judgmental listener and a true friend.

Friends are people with keys to your heart. Thank you for holding the key and keeping it safe!

Every time I need support in life, you're always there standing behind me. So good to have you in my life, thank you for being my best friends! Thanks for sharing an awesome and crazy friendship that always makes me smile and never let me down.

Though we've grown up, I still remember those sweet and naughty memories of our friendship. I don't think I would have been able to make it so far without your love, care, support, kindness, generosity, and every little or big thing. I love you guys, Thanks for everything, my best buddies!

Dearest former teachers,

As a former student and a friend. Too often, we climb through life without a look back to express our connection with others and our gratitude for their presence in our lives. You engage, inspire, and empower your students daily, and I wanted you to know that we notice how much you care.

You don't just try to figure out how to get information into their heads. You care about your students as people. Your class was always an environment where I was eager to express myself! You made me feel like you cared about what I had to say and valued my strengths and unique abilities instead of just focusing on how you could erase my weaknesses. You were excited to hear what I had to say, and I loved it when you said you learned something new from me or you'd tell me I asked a question that made you think.

Thank you for your time, your patience, and your realness. Thank you for encouraging me, supporting me, and caring about me. Thank you for seeing me as a partner in education, as someone who can teach others and learn. Thank you for inspiring me to learn and to help others the way you have. With my deepest gratitude.

Lastly, I offer my sincere thanks to all of you—all the readers of this book. It is because of you that I have had the opportunity to bring forth my realizations and understandings about our journey through life. I hope you enjoy my friendly humble attempt to pass on the wisdom that was given to me by my elders and teachers.

Table of Contents

Chapter – 01
Know who you are?

(Get to know the stranger living inside you)

You know what? The hardest person to get to know isn't a stranger. The hardest person to get to know is in the same room with you at all times. That damn person is yourself, nobody else. It can be tough to get to know your inner feelings and your most profound dreams, but there are ways to uncover this stranger's true self.

You spend more time with yourself than anyone else. Am I right? But tell me one thing mate, how well do you know yourself? You can say, finding yourself is not easy. But it's an important part of knowing one's self. Here's how to understand yourself better.

Sometimes you might find yourself doing things even though you're not quite sure why are you doing this. Our subconscious controls a huge amount of our behaviour and thus, the reasoning behind many of our decisions in life can be shrouded in mystery. However, if you know how to look, you can gain a greater understanding of yourself: why you make the decisions that you do, what makes you happy, and how you might change for the better. Do you get what I'm trying to say here, my friend?

Self-reflection builds self-awareness, but only through intention and dedication. This means you must regularly press "pause" on your busy life to create time and space to sit peacefully to sift through your thoughts and interactions to scrutinize them without judgment or condemnation.

Why is knowing SELF is important?

The value of self-understanding lies in its power to help identify what's working well in your life and develop insight into what isn't and why it's not. Isn't it?

Without the self-discovery that comes from introspection, you can become stuck in a routine that's neither productive nor inspiring and its literally kind of boring and lazy. You may not understand why you're dissatisfied or what you can do to improve your circumstances if you don't know what you truly want.

self-understanding seems like an intensely personal process, but embarking on a journey of introspection practice doesn't have to be intimidating. Simply taking five minutes in the evening to review your day and evaluate what worked for you and what didn't can set you on the path to self-development. Adopting this small change to your day-to-day routine can improve your well-being, and mental health and strengthen your relationships, make you a better leader tomorrow, and help you gain traction in your personal and professional development. You have nothing to lose from settling in and starting your self-understanding journey.

When setting out to discover yourself, start slowly. To grow, you need to confront both the good and bad aspects of your nature, but self-examination shouldn't lead to anxiety, stress, or depression. Majorly you should understand this point.

Step back and re-centre if you ever find yourself overthinking and beating yourself up over things that went wrong. The point of introspection isn't judgment and condemnation, but understanding and connecting with your sense of self.

Incorporate self-discovery into your daily, weekly, and monthly routines with some simple tips. Choose a time of day that's typically quiet and worry-free. For some people, it's when they wake up, and others go to bed. Whatever routine you set, stick to it — you won't see the same results if your self-reflection is inconsistent or approached without authenticity.

These are Some effective ways to approach the process of self-validation. Start with just one, testing the techniques until you find what works for you. Am I right?

1) Evaluate your strengths and weaknesses.

You can come to a better understanding of **who you are** and what is most important to you by thinking about your strengths and weaknesses. Importantly, you'll want to compare your perception of your strengths and weaknesses to the strengths and weaknesses identified by your friends, family, and co-workers. The things that they see that you don't can tell you a lot about yourself and how you see yourself.

- ➤ Examples of strengths include **determination, devotion, self-discipline, thoughtfulness, decisiveness, patience, diplomacy, communication skills, and imagination or creativity.**

- ➤ Examples of weaknesses include **close-mindedness, self-centeredness, difficulty perceiving reality, judgement of others, and issues with control.**

2) Don't Try to Fit in and Give you a fresh perspective

Remember one thing my friend, not everyone is going to like you. You may be the most popular super star on the planet, but someone won't like you. Don't try to fit in with everyone. Don't flex yourself to be like everyone else around you so that you can fit in a particular circle. **Be yourself, so you don't lose yourself.** When you realize the feeling of not fitting in, be **proud** that you're not like the rest of the **crowd.** Lead your own circle and this will help you understand yourself a bit better.

When you're in the moment, emotion can cloud your judgment, making a bad situation seem worse than it is. **Self-validation lets you re-evaluate your circumstances calmly and rationally to process what's happening and find a solution with greater clarity.**

Look at how you've changed. Look at your past and think about how what has happened to you over your lifetime has affected how you act and think today. Looking at how you've changed as a person can reveal a lot about why you act the way that you do, because our current behaviours are built on our past experiences.

3) Help understand yourself.

Self-validation grants insight into your authentic self, allowing you to really grasp why you make certain choices and what makes you truly happy. When you identify your priorities, you can pursue them without doubt and confusion. You can be confident that you know what you want and what's best for you.

4) Listen to Your Positive Inner Voice

Your inner voice judges you more than it does anyone else. It often hurts us because we only listen to the wrong things it tells us. It's okay to listen to the inner voices but take away the negative words. Listen to the good things it tells you about yourself. Your inner voice might stand in the way of your happiness because it often tells us we don't look good enough, work hard enough, or aren't good enough for the world. Take out the bullying mate, and listen only to the positive thoughts, I repeat again **only positive thoughts.**

5) Maintain Notes

Speaking of your inner voice, transfer it to **notes.** You can find and know yourself on the deepest level by taking notes. There are no rules when you're writing. Let your inner voice guide you to write what you feel and how you feel. You have to be quiet and really dig in when you begin to write. No one else is going to read these words, so you don't have to worry about damn people or anyone judging you. Your true self can pour into the pages because it's all about you. Listen to your deepest thoughts and read your most profound words to uncover your real inner voice that is more important.

6) Find Your Patterns in Life

Find the repeating patterns in your life. Ask yourself about your habits in relationships, both personal and professional. If your relationships with friends and loved ones often suffer, ask yourself what you are repeatedly doing that causes these failures and feeling broken. If you keep getting close to your professional dreams but fail, then ask yourself what you are doing wrong each time. Repetitive situations and conflicts often keep us from achieving our goals in life. Once we figure out what is going wrong in your way, we can work to fix these bloody wrongs. We can rise above the mistakes and move toward situations positively. We are all human we make some wrong deeds it's all okay and it's all normal to face it, but important role is to correct them all from wrong to right behaviours.

7) Get to Know Your Body

Getting to know yourself doesn't have to only be about your psychological self. You can also get to know your physical self. This isn't about all of your flaws. This is about getting to identify ways to push yourself physically. You need to be in tune with your body so you know what it can do. While you're figuring this out, find out ways to love those flaws as well

8) Listen to Your Automatic Thoughts

Many times our automatic thoughts are negative or even irrational. You may choose to fall into these negative thoughts accepting them as truth. You then start to have a bad day and see yourself in a negative light. When you have a positive self-value, you begin catching negative thoughts and turning them around. You can redirect your mind when you hear automatic negative thoughts. When you hear negative thoughts, take a deep breath, and challenge them. Know when they're irrational. Know when they're bad for your mind. You know you're good enough. Tell this to yourself over and over, so the positive slowly takes over the negative automatic thoughts.

9) Sense of well-being and Examine your priorities.

Understanding your priorities and values helps you establish healthy boundaries that protect your mental health and build self-esteem. When you have an intimate understanding of what inspires, upsets, and drives you, you can better prepare yourself for negative reactions and find positive motivators to push you forward. That you think is most important in life and in your day-to-day interactions can tell you a lot about yourself. Think about your priorities, compare them to the priorities of other people you respect, and think what your conclusions say about you. Of course, you need to be open to the idea that you might not have your priorities in the best order (many people don't), which can also teach you a lot about yourself.

10) Uncover Your Hobbies

Do you know what you enjoy doing for fun? Do you just go along with the grain and do whatever everyone else is doing? Take time to figure out what it is that you love to do. You might uncover the fact you genuinely love hiking and hate painting. You might've gone bowling with friends a million times, yet didn't enjoy it. Try out other activities like yoga or a spin class. You might love cooking, so try cooking classes. A little experimenting might uncover a whole new level of yourself.

11) Be honest with yourself.

We lie to ourselves a lot more than we'd like to think about sometimes. We'll help ourselves to think that we made some questionable choices for noble or logical reasons, even when we were really just being vindictive or lazy. But hiding from the real reason behind our motives doesn't help us change and develop into better people. Remember: there's no point in lying to yourself. Even if you discover truths about yourself that you really don't like, this only gives you the opportunity to take those problems head on instead of just pretending like they don't exist.

12) Listen to what others say to and about you.

Sometimes, especially when we do bad things, others will try to warn us against those behaviours. We also have a tendency not to listen. Sometimes this is good, because lots of people will say things about you just because they want to hurt you and their comment will have no basis in fact. But sometimes what they say is a good, outsider's analysis of how you behave. Think about what people have said in the past and ask for some new opinions about your behaviour.

> For example, your sister might notice that you tend to exaggerate. But this is unintentional on your part, which can serve to show you that your perception of reality is a bit off.

> There's a big difference between evaluating what they say about you and letting that opinion control your life and actions. You shouldn't tailor your behaviour to suit other people unless it is having a significantly negative impact on your life (and even then, you might want to consider that your environment might be the problem, not your behaviour). Make changes because you want to change, not because someone else tells you that you should.

13) Improve your decision-making skills.

When you know what makes you tick, you're better prepared to make the right decisions for your future. You have the clarity you need to pursue your dreams while giving you the flexibility to respond to changing circumstances. You need to work on **decision-making skills**. This will build you.

14) Find Your Mission

Find your mission in life by figuring out the most meaningful times of your life. Think about the events that have shaped you as a person. How did they lead you to where you are today? How can they lead you to better satisfaction in life? It's good to uncover these answers, so you better understand some of the ways you handle things. You may have had traumatic experiences that cause you to handle everything in life a certain way. You may take little things from many different events in your life. Find your mission through these events.

15) Take time and experience life.

The best way to really get to know yourself, however, is to just experience life. Just like getting to know another person, understanding yourself takes time and you'll learn far more through experiencing life than by interviewing yourself and taking tests on yourself. You can try:

> ➤ Traveling. Traveling will put you in lots of different situations and test your ability to handle stress and adapt to change. You'll come to a greater understanding of your happiness, priorities, and dreams than you ever could just sitting in your same old boring life.

> ➤ Letting go of expectations. Let go of other people's expectations for you. Let go of your expectations for yourself. Let go of your expectations for what life should be like. When you do this, you'll be more open to seeing what new experiences might make you

happy and fulfilled. Life is a crazy roller-coaster and you're going to encounter a lot of things that scare you because they're new or different but don't close yourself to those experiences. They might make you happier than you've ever been.

Important notes to be Followed

Practice gratitude

Sit back and review what you're thankful for. Itemizing things that make you feel grateful is an excellent way to boost your mood and improve your outlook. Start by listing three things that made you happy during the day, and then scale backward.

Set your goals

Get specific and identify your goals. Write them down and use them as guidelines for your introspection activities. Mate, have you reached the milestones that will bring you closer to the desired outcome? Are there any thought patterns holding you back? Is there something you need to learn to progress? These questions and more are fuel for your self-reflection journey. Set goals and work on it. (you will learn more in goal setting chapter).

Have a conversation with yourself

Hearing your thoughts out loud can generate insight in ways that merely thinking about them can't. Self-talk forces you to clearly articulate your emotions, leading to a clearer understanding of what you're feeling at the time. It also helps you organize your thoughts logically to communicate them clearly to others. Make sense?

Get out into nature and reboot your mind

If you're having trouble getting into the frame of mind required for personal reflection, try getting out into nature. Spending time in the outdoors has a grounding effect, putting you in the moment by removing distractions and clearing your head so you can think. Reboot your mind.

It's also a wonderful way to remove yourself from an environment, like your home or office, that may contain triggers that distract you from the self-reflection process.

Take care of yourself. If not, you then who will?

It's essential to nurture yourself so you can love yourself. Practice self-care so you can get to know what motivates you. This could mean taking a warm bath with candles, going for a jog, or simply taking a nap. Refresh yourself, so you don't go crazy during the day. Challenges are a daily struggle, so you need to be at your peak self, so you know how to approach them.

Knowing your true self will lead to a higher level of success in all areas of your life. Being true to that person is one of the most important things you'll ever do in life. **Get to know the stranger living inside you,** and you'll be further ahead in life than most people.

Words of Affirmation

Tell yourself as much as possible that you are worth it. Give yourself the **positive push** so you can find the **goodness** within yourself. You'll begin to see all of the good things about yourself this way. Think about all of the great things about your life. Face the day with these affirmations.

Chapter – 02
Dealing with darkness

(Depression and Suicide)

Over the last five years, more than 40,000 students committed suicide in India. Last year, 8,492 students committed suicide. One student commits suicide every hour in India, and yet, we keep pretending like today's teenagers are anything from fragile to obsessed about their looks -- each of these blame games makes diagnosis and treatment of teenage depression even more difficult.

Mental health issues that students are facing today

As we speak there is one suicide attempt every three seconds and one death by suicide every forty seconds by our youth. These statistics alone are alarming enough to take cognizance of the fact that mental health among students is going to be the next crisis.

Paying attention to students' mental health is the need of the hour. According to a study published in the Asian Journal of Psychiatry, over 53% of Indian university students suffer from moderate to extremely severe depression. Our studies show that 74% of Indian students suffer from high to severe stress.

The Covid-19 pandemic and lockdown haven't been kind to our student population. They are amongst the worst hit emotionally -- 58% of Indian college students experienced a significant increase in their stress levels and severe deterioration in their emotions of anger, anxiety, loneliness, hopelessness, and happiness.

As per WHO- Globally, close to 800 000 people die by suicide every year; that's one person every 40 seconds. For each suicide, there are more than 20 suicide attempts.

While the link between suicide and mental disorders (in particular, depression and alcohol use disorders) is well established, many suicides happen impulsively in moments of crisis. Risk factors include the experience of loss, loneliness, discrimination, a relationship break-up, financial problems, chronic pain and illness, violence, abuse, and conflict or other humanitarian emergencies. The strongest risk factor for suicide is a previous suicide attempt.

Suicide is an emerging and serious public health issue in India. However, it is preventable with timely, evidence-based and often low-cost interventions. The suicide mortality rate per 100 000 populations in 2016 was 16.5, while the global average was 10.5 per 100 000. The most vulnerable are the 15-29-year old's, the elderly, and persons with special needs.

The Mental Healthcare Act of 2017 decriminalizes suicide, assuring adequate medical relief to those attempting it. This landmark development ensures dignity and a humane perspective on the issue. The National Mental Health Programme and Health and Wellness Centres under the **Ayushman Bharat Program** are efforts to provide quality care at the primary health care level. De-addiction centres and rehabilitation services are also available.

A strengthened system for quality data on suicides (attempted and deaths) from vital registration, hospital-based systems and other surveys for formulating policies and subsequent monitoring are effective suicide prevention initiatives. Strengthening life-skill training and counselling in educational institutions, workplaces etc. further supplement prevention policies.

In India, pesticides, firearms, self-hanging, and jumping off bridges and in front of trains are the major means by which suicide is attempted. Policies limiting access to pesticides, and firearms and putting barriers on bridges and railway platforms could be some of the preventive options. In addition, counselling services and creating destigmatized platforms for discussion around these taboo subjects could be considered.

Let me tell you the story which made me write this chapter here. In the year of 2020, the deadliest pandemic phase was in India, everybody started getting locked in their own spaces due to coronavirus LOCKDOWN, in the crises of covid phase many people lost their jobs and loved ones, it's a kind of black hole for the people who experienced it closely.

At that time many people struggled to get a peaceful life. It was the biggest disturbance, mental fear of covid and lay off in the work area. Due to this kind of situation and people were falling mentally sick at one place and there is no option to-do with.

it's hard to say one of my dear friends that he was laid off from his job. And right after that, he tried everywhere to fit into a new job, due to the market breakdown cause of covid.

For several months he spent his life without earning. Do you know in our society how they treat if a man loses his job? they start treating him as the biggest loser in his life. Being a man isn't easy too and he tried to express his pain to his relatives and his society. Do you know the ugly thing of this society is instead of motivating him and supporting him they were starting feeding him negative thoughts and hatred. Here, we need to understand one thing. This society and relatives are not going to feed us food when we don't have any, but obviously, they are going to feed your mind with negativity. We should not lose hope and we should keep faith in ourselves.

After going through a dark phase with all the circumstances and majorly when his loved ones failed to understand him and when he failed to understand himself, he had lost his control over emotional pain and societal pressures. My heart shakes to write this, but I have to write to get on paper how really cruel society is. One day he decided to end his life leaving a message to society **"I have failed but never judge a man with his abilities. I failed to make you understand but my death is going to realise you what you have done to me"**.

I lost my dear friend I was unware of what and all he had been through, the moment I got the news I was in shock that could able to believe that the man who is used to speak every time with the warm smile and kindness in his heart. if I think of him still appears his smiling face. Damn I can't forget it. **We need to learn more what is depression and how to overcome?**

What is depression?

Feeling sad is a normal reaction to experiences that are stressful or upsetting. However, when these feelings go on for a long time, interfere with your life or make you feel unlike your usual self, you might have depression.

Most people, young people as well as adults, feel low, sad or `blue' occasionally, this is a normal reaction to experiences that are stressful or upsetting.

When these feelings continue over a period of time, or take over and get in the way of your normal daily life, they can become an illness. This illness is called `depression'.

Depression is one of the most common emotional problems around the world; the good news is that it is also one of the most treatable. In fact, 80% of people who receive treatment for depression go on to have a better quality of life – they feel better and enjoy themselves in a way that they weren't able to before. And 20% of the people fail to come out from the depression and end up their life.

I want to give this message to those who are willing to give up on their life.

Hey Mate! It's okay to talk about the things you feel, about your depression, your anxiety and your stress and all the things you worry about, it's okay to struggle with these things in order to how to deal with it. to not to know where to begin or how to deal with it or how to heal, it's all okay my friend but don't keep it everything inside you. Talk about how you feel and what you feel, be honest and be open about it. It's okay to break down in tears, this is how you change, and this is how you will heal, by talking about it and by letting the people who care about you to know, what it is your holding so far. Don't bottle up inside in your heart, don't bury it and let it out and let the sunlight in like this your journey begins, yeah like this properly you grow.

Find someone who will help you when you are in the dark room, who will relive the anxiety, not add to on you. Someone will who will help to calm the chaos and stress and depression. Not to give you more of it. and someone who soothes the soul. who helps you to soften of the world a bit, not to add you on the hard edges, who will make your pain and problems a little bearable, more tolerable, someone who makes your path easy. These are the kind of people you need. The ones who help you when you need them the most, who make your heart sing, the ones who make you feel the sun a little warmer than it Is. The one who give love without effort. Find them and follow them.

Buddy! In case if you are in the situation don't ever think of ending life for any situation, and I would like to say that you are really a brave and strong person because life gives you every reason to give up and you still rise, you shine and you pick yourself up and move forward with a wide smile. That's how you make the world better. Depression is like a real battle you have to win here like a warrior and don't be a coward and end your beautiful, think about your family and loved ones and come back as a better person.

Friendly reminder my friend! Whatever it is that is causing you pain and all of this stress. All of this anxiety, worries, depressions will pass, and you will survive like a monster and move on with experiences, as you always have a bad day, and tomorrow is a new one. Embrace the beauty of positivity and stay strong. No one is really breaks you, and you think you are broken inside but actually, you are not. In the same way you think you are lost but you are really just discovering who really you are.

As a young person with depression, you may experience problems not only with how you feel but also with how you behave. This can cause difficulties at home and at the work area, as well as in relationships with your family and loved ones.

Some young people start taking risks. These can include missing collage or work place, harming themselves through misusing drugs or alcohol, or having inappropriate sexual relationships. Sometimes young people with depression may self-harm, or try to kill themselves. If you are considering harming yourself, you should speak to someone you trust straight away.

A small number of young people with depression may develop 'psychotic' symptoms like hearing voices or believing that someone is trying to harm them. Some young people have periods of having a very low mood, followed by periods of having a very high mood. This might be a sign that you have bipolar disorder.

Depression in young people

What are the causes of depression in young people?

There is no one single factor that will lead to the onset of depression, genes and family tendencies can deter whether someone is likely to be more susceptible to depression but there are also many other factors that can act as potential triggers which may prompt depression; one of which is that of the pressure of modern life on young people.

In our modern society, young people are fed information which puts pressure on them to meet needs that are often unrealistic. They are inundated with images as to how they are meant to look, what they are meant to have and how they are meant to behave, all based on the assumption that this is important to live. If young people feel that they do not meet the images that are portrayed to them via the media or peers, they can often feel different, that they are not good enough or disadvantaged which, if not dealt with appropriately, can lead to depression as well as problems with self-esteem, and confidence.

School can be a positive setting for learning, growth and development for many young people but it can also be a place where young people struggle in terms of fitting in, keeping up with a heavy workload, performance pressures and exam stress. Failing an important exam at school can cause great frustration and may lead to depressed feelings. Bullying is also an issue that unfortunately affects many young people. Bullying can seriously affect a young person's mental and physical health. It can lead to feelings of anxiety, low self-esteem and poor concentration. The transition from one school to another or the leaving of school can also act as a trigger for the onset of depression.

Stressful relationships can also act as triggers for depression. For some young people, a negative, stressful or unhappy family atmosphere can affect their self-esteem and lead to depression. Conflict within the family, divorce or separation leading to a change in living arrangements can lead to feelings of insecurity, guilt, anger, rejection or a sense of loss. Poverty, abuse and violence within the family are also key contributors. Difficulties in making and maintaining friendships or relationships, can lead to low self-esteem and a loss of confidence which in turn makes it more difficult for the young person to find someone they feel comfortable with to share their worries.

Other triggers that have been identified in the lives of young people that may lead to the onset of depression include; the loss of a loved one, physical illness of self or a loved one, living with a parent or relative who has depression, being subject to physical or emotional abuse, weight gain, something embarrassing happening or a financial setback.

How to recognize signs of depression in young people?

It is not always easy to recognize the signs of depression in young people. Young people face many challenges as they find their way in life but most balance their common troubles with good friendships, success in school/college or outside activities and develop a strong sense of self. Certain negative behaviours are to be expected, such as occasional bad moods and acting out, however, depression is something different. Depression can lead to dramatic long-term changes in personality, mood and behaviour. Certain signs can help to identify whether a young person is suffering from depression, whilst considering these signs it is also important to acknowledge how long the symptoms have been present, their severity and the degree to which the young person is acting in a different manner to his or her usual self. Some signs of depression in young people include:

How do I know if I have depression?

Some of the symptoms of depression can include:

- being moody and irritable - easily upset, angry or tearful
- having less energy than usual
- not enjoying activities that you previously enjoyed
- becoming withdrawn - avoiding friends, family, school and regular activities

- feeling guilty or bad, being self-critical and blaming or hating yourself
- feeling hopeless and wanting to die
- finding it difficult to concentrate
- not looking after your personal appearance or your personal self-care
- changes in sleep pattern - sleeping too little or too much, and feeling tired
- losing interest in eating, not feeling hungry, eating too little or too much
- unexplained aches and pains, such as headaches or stomach aches
- taking risks or harming yourself

If you have experienced more than one of these signs and have had them persistently for more than two weeks, it might mean that you are depressed.

How to protect the mental health of students and youth at three levels?

It is pertinent that we must all come together as a country and as a community to really protect our youth, at 3 levels.

1. Individual level:

We need to empower our youth and help them become more resilient individuals. There are many ways to facilitate this.

For this, institutions must introduce stress management training, physical activity programmes, and e-courses for self-help, and of course, professional therapy support.

2. Community level:

These consist of communities like academic course batches, etc. academic institutes must make it mandatory for their respective communities including students to undergo training in psychological first aid and suicide gatekeeping.

The goal here is to build peer support and a caring community culture.

3. Organizational level:

Whether it be at the academic institutional level, or at the governmental level, we need to make sure that youth mental health is the agenda at the leadership level.

It's our responsibility as a country and as a community to protect our youth, to be there for them in their toughest times. We need to empower our students to be resilient well-rounded adults.

What to do if a person is depressed?

If you do suspect a young person as having depression, it is important to find support immediately, recovery is much quicker in those who feel supported by those around them whether a family member, true friend, counsellor or doctor.

In supporting a young person experiencing depression there are positive steps that you can take to help and provide support. For instance:

> ➢ Encourage them to talk about their feelings making sure that it is clear to the young person that you are willing to provide whatever support is necessary

- ➤ Take an understanding approach and listen carefully to what the young person is saying, if you criticize or pass judgement the young person will feel that you do not take their emotions seriously and will refuse to talk on the matter in the future
- ➤ Avoid comments like, "Snap out of it", "Get your act together" as this can strengthen feelings of self-blame and low self-esteem
- ➤ Learn about depression, the more you know the better equipped you will be to help
- ➤ Research the sources of support that are available, offer to go with them to a doctor's appointment or to speak to someone else.
- ➤ Encourage the young person to take part in physical activity, exercise such as walking the dog can help alleviate the symptoms of depression
- ➤ It is also important to look after your own mental health. Whilst it is important to be there for a young person, don't try and cope with everything on your own. Getting help and support will make things easier for both you and your young person.

Medical Treatment and how to overcome?

If you feel that your person is showing signs that they are depressed, it is important to seek professional help in order for a diagnosis to be made. A doctor will take note of how long the young person has been showing symptoms of depression, the extent to which the symptoms are interfering with their daily life and any changes in behavior. The doctor will also enquire as to whether or not there is a family history of depression or a mental health disorder. Your doctor may prescribe some medication to ease the young person's symptoms or recommend other specialist services such as counselling and talking therapies.

Whilst depression can be a difficult condition to live with for the individual and the immediate family and friends, it is important to remember that depression can be treated and individuals have a good chance of making a full recovery when provided with the appropriate treatment and support.

If you are reading this, I will tell you that it's very difficult to move forward holding the mountain on your shoulders, it's time to release the weight which is dragging you back. Say this to yourself I am learning each and every day to allow the space between where I am and where I want to be and inspires me and not terrify me.

Make practice of asking for what you really want. No self-imposed guilt. No Self-imposed shame. Do not be afraid to voice what you desire or what you really deserve. Be, Live, Enjoy.

It's time for you to start taking the necessary steps and actions to become the version of yourself that you can't stop dreaming about. You know many peoples be burden on your goals, they come and feed all the negative thoughts in your head, if your voice in your head is mean to you, remember that someone manipulated that voice and installed it in you. Kill that fake voice and you must find yours. You know the ocean can't sink a ship unless it gets inside the ship, negativity can't sink you unless it gets inside you.

Find such a friends like who wants to bring the very best in you. With true friend's conversation is the best therapy, speaking everything out from heart, sometimes, that all you need to pull out of the darkness. Someone who willing to understand without judging you, someone who is willing to listen all your problems, someone who willing to stay by you side, no matter how tough it gets.

Visualize Good Things

You should also try to focus on the good things in your life. When you're feeling down, it can be helpful to take a few minutes every day to visualize something positive. This could be something like spending time with friends or family, traveling, or simply enjoying a quiet moment at home.

See Life in Different Ways

You should also try to accept that not everything in life is going to go your way. When you're feeling down, it can be tough to see the good in things, but it's important to remember that bad days happen to everyone. Try to focus on the positives, even when things are tough.

Set Boundaries

You can also try to set boundaries in your relationships. This means being honest with the people in your life about what you can and cannot handle. It's important to be considerate of others, but you also need to take care of yourself. You can try saying no to things that you don't have the energy for or setting limits on how much time you spend with certain people.

See Positives in Life

You can also try on seeing positive things in life. It's not always going to be easy, but it can help you feel better in the long run. When you're feeling down, try to take a few minutes every day to think about something positive. This could be something like your favourite thing about yourself, a happy memory, or something good that's happening in your life right now.

LET'S TALK ABOUT THE SUICIDE AND IT EFFECTS ON THE FAMILY AND LOVED ONES

When someone dies by suicide, the people impacted most dramatically are those closest to the person who died family, friends, co-workers, classmates etc. As a result, the people who interacted regularly with the individual who ended their life will miss the physical presence of that person and typically feel the loss most intimately.

Stigma and the Effects of Suicide in Family and Friends

When a person dies, societally, others generally offer empathy and compassion, but when a person dies by suicide, there is a stigma around that death and people often treat the loved ones of the person who committed suicide differently. Loved ones can be very afraid to talk about the suicide for fear of judgment and condemnation – being blamed for the suicide of their family member or friend. Because of this, one effect of suicide on family and friends can be extreme isolation.

Effects of Suicide on Family and Friends

Learning that a loved one has died by suicide can absolutely be traumatic. In addition to all the feelings that anyone would feel about the death of a loved one, when the death is a suicide, there are additional feelings like:

> Extreme guilt for not preventing the suicide

> Failure because a person they loved felt unloved and completed suicide

> Anger or resentment at the person who chose to take his or her own life

> Confusion

> Distress over unresolved issues (many of which often exist in families where one person has a mental illness, which is common in people who die by suicide)

The person who kill themselves are just transfer their pain to family members, they think and kill them cause to end the issues which they were suffering for eventually they transfer that emotional pain to mother and father. Before ending your precious like sit and think about innocent faces of your parents. They are living on this earth just because of you. You are the light to the family and don't take it off your family's light. You will never know what they have been go through once you put off your life to the nature! It's very difficult to handle this situation to your family. Mate, we born only once and we live every moment, but think that every problem has a solution, every puzzle has its own tricks to solve so please do have a glance on your mother and father before taking such a coward decision. This society ppl will forget your existence with short time of period, but your family and loved ones they suffer until they die. Don't escape from the reality giving the unmeaning full answers, stand with your true loved ones try to face and be an example to this society.

The ultimate betrayal is always the betrayal of the self. Read it once before thinking of end yourself

Forgive the part of you that ignored the information, you were receiving through your intuition, the body nudges and your own inner guidance. Priorities your own mental health and happiness even when its inconvenient for others. You are not how other people see you and it's all okay. That you are not who you thought you would be either let go of what wants to leave as long as you don't lose yourself, you are good. You know it's all about falling in love with yourself and sharing that love, Joy with someone who really appreciates you. It's time to create a positive vibe around you.

Strengths also looks like.

➤ Letting go of what no longer serves you.

➤ Breaking to rebuild yourself fir better tomorrow.

➤ Transcending negativity

➤ Positive intentions

➤ Taking dynamic moves towards positivity

➤ Smiling and inner joy

➤ Trusting the process

➤ Alone Self-care time

➤ Cutting off the toxic people.

You know what my friend?

➤ It's okay to feel alone.

➤ It's okay to feel you are lost in the ocean.

➤ It's okay to feel empty and broken.

For everything lonely finds its company. Everything lost is meant to be found, everything empty is meant to gets filled, eventually broken parts will be fixed.

Let's see will think like this my mate, think about all the terrible times you have lived through, just think about how they were and how it's all passed. You are a warrior on the battlefield, you have to go through hell to find heaven, likewise you must break in order to find yourself whole again.

Buddy! you are really a brave and strong person because life gives you every reason to give up and you still, you rise, you shine and you pick yourself up and move forward with a wide smile. That's how you make the world better.

Water your bad days with love and patience, watch as flowers grow from it tomorrow. In this era people do spend entire day looking at their mobiles and laptop screens they just attached to the unrealistic world where they don't exist. You have to keep those devices aside and Think about what you want, not what you don't want, guard your thoughts carefully, because they create your experiences. Sometimes you have to take a pause to appreciate yourself and how you have come. Remember self-appreciation is also a major key to kick start your inner energy.

Just say with me: I'm going to make my parents proud and I will never give up on this beautiful life, I'm a warrior and not a worrier, this battle is mine, I come up with my victory.

Higher states of vibration will help you to feel good, which means you can manifest more good things in your life.

Your aim is to feel better by vibrating higher, there are many life style habits that will help you to do this and bring you closer to a loving and joyful state.

You can change your emotional state through all sorts of activities that will rise our vibration, some of which have a lasting effect while others may make you feel good only in that moment. You are going to explore in upcoming chapters.

Chapter – 03
Climate of opinion

(How to Deal with Social Pressure and Follow Your Own way)

Do you ever feel that there is always some sort of pressure on you? No matter how "relaxed" you are, there is always something to fix. In my opinion, in today's society, there are unneeded pressures on everyone, in this case, the millennials of my generation. It all started as early as kindergarten; you were in a new environment apart from your parents and you always tried to seek attention from the kids around you. In middle school, there is an un-relentless pressure of trying to fit in. This sadly brings kids into anxiety and depression

In high school, the heartaches and headaches you get from stressing yourself out are brutal. The number one pressure I can think of in high school is grades, the ability to get the best grades to get into the perfect college in order to get that perfect, utopian future.

This pressure stays with individuals to become perfectionists. In life, no one is perfect, everyone makes mistakes and that's what makes us human. Getting good grades is important but if you are incapable of getting the 1st rank, and you are trying your best, that's all you can ask for and do. Employers and other people don't only look at your Grades, they look at how much effort you put in and how involved you are.

When you are in college you have a lot more freedom to be whom you want to be without all the cliques of high school. However, there are still pressures that a lot of college students face.

In general, the media and society create a false idealistic person that everyone needs to be. Reality shows and movies show the "best of the best" but these people are just acting, that's not who they are. Be yourself, everyone else is taken. Don't waste your time trying to be that cool kid or that actor you see on TV; look at them as your role model if anything and base your goals on them. Stick to your core foundations and don't let anyone tell you otherwise, because you are the best you, you can be. And remember, always have hope.

I rarely check out the news and a few days back I was scrolling social media, I read the news which made me feel bring this in front of you people and understand the scenario.

News is 10th Class Girl Ends Life Owing to Board Exam Stress, wrote 'Can't Score Over 95%' In Suicide Note.

In the suicide note, the 15-year-old girl wrote - 'I am sorry Mummy and Pappa. I can't do this...

Where are we heading when our young generation who must be full of life & vigour decide to take their life because he/she couldn't cope up with their studies?

Are we pressurizing our kids way too much, more than what they can handle? In a recent case, coming in from Rajasthan, a class 10th student, committed suicide, leaving behind a suicide note in which she mentioned the hard reality of the pressure that students are facing these days. The girl, identified as Khushbu Meena (15) was preparing for her board exams, but couldn't handle the extreme pressure to score well. In the note, she stated that she was tense due to her 10th-class board exams and that she was unable to handle the pressure of scoring more than 95% in exams.

According to the reports, the 15-year-old girl committed suicide by hanging herself with a rope when her parents were not at home. In the note, she wrote: **"I am sorry Mummy and Pappa. I can't do this. I feel pressured due to the 10th board exams. I won't be able to score more than 95% on the exams. I love you Papa, Mummy, and Rishabh. I am so sorry."**

How to Help Your Child Reduce Exam Stress?

It is important for the child to score well if he/she wants to reach their goals. But is it so much important that the student should start feeling like it is a burden on her? Education is important, but not at the cost of someone's life. A child should never feel stress in the worse way possible, especially when the exams are nearing. And who can help these kids do that? Their family.

As a parent, here are some ways you can help your child deal with extra stress:

> - Try to communicate with your child as much as possible.
> - Do not make comparisons between how your child is preparing and how other kids are preparing.
> - Teach your children relaxing skills.
> - Help your child manage stress.
> - Make sure your child is eating well.

- ➤ Do not add to the pressure.
- ➤ If possible, try to help your child focus on good things when he/she is not studying.
- ➤ Warning Signs of Suicidal Behavior

Suicidal thoughts can be extremely bad for a child. As a parent, it is important that your kid is preparing for the exams in a healthy way. Too much pressure and stress can sometimes make the student feel worthless, and that sometimes trigger **suicidal thoughts** in their mind. Here are some warning signs a parent should always look out for:

- ➤ Talking about wanting to die
- ➤ Talking about feeling worthless, hopeless and empty
- ➤ Mentioning strong feelings of guilt and shame
- ➤ Thinking or talking about not having a reason to live
- ➤ Social withdrawal and isolation
- ➤ Giving away personal items to others
- ➤ Saying goodbye to friends and family (texts, or actions)

It is important that you encourage your child, and spread positive vibes around them during their exam days. It may look easy for others, but the stress and anxiety that comes with board exams are real, and only those who are with the child (student), can only help them stay strong.

Let's understand about social pressure

Social pressure is the direct influence of other people on your thoughts, desires, and actions. It's the feeling that you should live your life according to other people's narratives, following a path that's considered "acceptable" by modern society. Social pressure confines us to a box, limiting the options of what's considered a "successful life." We've all been there, watching our friends enter the corporate workforce, get married, have children, and more.

But social pressure isn't an external force exerted by society in an attempt to keep you confined to a path you ultimately don't want. Rather, it's internal pressure you put on yourself based on your subconscious need to fit in with those around you. This means that we have the power to break social norms and live the lives that make us truly happy. we'll discuss the ways in which you can overcome your feelings of social pressure in order to live your best life.

The Desire to Fit In

Social pressure typically encourages people to try to fit in with those around them. Sometimes fitting in may come naturally, but in other cases, a person may feel the need to change their views, choices, and outlooks to avoid being the odd one out. Sometimes, social pressure can encourage positive changes, but sometimes it can encourage negative and harmful behaviours.

It is possible that the human desire to fit in with a given group has an evolutionary basis. As a species, human beings can be largely dependent on one another and usually survive best when living in a community with others. In the process of growing up, children learn a great deal of cultural and social information, which usually includes learning to follow the norms of their society. Managing one's attitudes and behaviours to stay connected to the community can therefore be a survival strategy to help us achieve adulthood successfully and potentially provide benefits such as friendship, having potential mates, helping with raising children, and getting resources that we need to live.

1- The majority is often wrong

Social pressure is often a powerful force because when several people show disapproval towards something we do, we automatically assume they are right and we are wrong since we are alone and they are many. Our minds tend to operate on the principle that the majority is always correct.

However, in practice, that is frequently not true. In fact, let's face it: **most people don't really know what they're talking about most of the time.** They believe various ideas simply because they've been exposed to them thousands of times from a young age and they never bothered to question them; then they go through life following those ideas, living unimpressive lives, and expecting others to do the same.

So when you consider this, it makes no sense to give authority to an idea just because a lot of people believe it. If anything, it's probably a sign it's a flawed idea. This is something to always bear in mind when confronted with social pressure.

Sometimes your goals and behaviors, even though they make rational sense, will come into conflict with the way others would like you to act and live. When this happens, such people may try to make you conform using emotional tools such as sarcasm, criticism, withdrawal of approval, threats or rejection.

The use of such tools by a number of people to exert influence over you is what's known as social pressure. **It's a force meant to make you conform to the will of others** around you and, more broadly, to the standards of society.

I've had many conversations with people who've made numerous sacrifices in life due to social pressure. Almost without exception, when they look back, they regret having given in to the desires of others instead of doing what they truly wanted to do.

This is why it's key to know how to deal with social pressure. It frees you to follow your own path in life and do so without any shame. With this in mind, I'd like to give you a few practical ideas:

2- Clearly Define Your "Why?"

One of the biggest issues with social pressure is that people often don't have a firm understand of what drives them. Instead, they default to the things that society says should drive us - money, job titles, material possessions, and cheap thrills. But is that what drives you personally? Be honest with yourself. I'm sure it's not.

However, if you're unable to define what drives you, it's easy to follow the narrative that other people say results in "success." But what if the success of one person doesn't result in the success of the other? What if the goals of your friend are the opposite of what you truly want deep down inside? Well, if you follow that opposite path, you might seem successful in the traditional sense, but you'll feel incongruent with your true self, resulting in unhappiness.

This is why it's extremely important to clearly define your "why." Your why is the underlying reason for all of your actions. For example, the fact that you want to be a touring musician may be the why that causes you to go to music school rather than a traditional college. If you want to be an entrepreneur, business owners might be the why that forces you to drop out of college and take an entry-level job with an interesting startup that'll teach you how to scale a company.

If you know what your why is, it becomes much easier to say "no" when your social pressure rears its ugly head. No one can see the vision for your life, but if you can't see it either, then there's no chance that you'll be able to live it. For this reason, when you want to overcome social pressure, you need to have a firm understanding of the "why" that drives your actions, so that when someone tries to influence you in another direction, you can identify right away that it's not the right direction for you.

3- Ask yourself first

Before automatically believing what others say is correct, ask yourself what you think about it. Do you agree with their values and views? If not, always prioritize your own perspective.

For example, if a friend tells you that not drinking alcohol is for boring people or that you should lose weight to be attractive, or your partner says that you should move in together, stop and think. Ask yourself if you agree with them. Do you really want to drink, lose weight, or move in with your partner?

You must give yourself the space to clarify your own ideas and priorities. Without this foundation, you'll get carried away by what others suggest to you.

4- Find People Who Accept You as You Are

The fact many people don't approve of what you do or how you do it doesn't mean that all of humanity is rejecting you. But it can often feel that way; unless there are also people in your life who accept you the way you are.

These people can be either

A) like-minded people, who are similar to you in goals and behavior, or B) open-minded people, who have a lot of tolerance towards diversity.

Such people are great because **they confirm that being true to yourself is not a death sentence for your social life**. It's reassuring to know that you can follow your path, and even though many will object, some people are fine with it and will keep being your friends.

If you lack such people in your social circle, I encourage you wholeheartedly to find them and keep them close. Get involved in social events, meet new people, get to know them better and spot the ones who accept you as you are. Make friends with such people and foster those friendships. For an unconventional person in particular, they are priceless.

Once you've learned to deal with it, social pressure is really no big deal. All that will truly matter to you is that you understand why you want to do what you want to do, and it feels right to you.

You'll feel motivated to follow your own path and you won't be distracted by herd-like opposition. You'll live true to yourself and you'll be proud of yourself for it.

Chapter – 04
Deal with a negative mind

(How to Deal with negative people)

We all seem to have some people who never be happy. They **keep** about things, but no matter what solution you suggest, they will find a reason why it won't work. **Although you can never suggest a "workable" solution.**

How about that friend who always discourages you from reaching your goals because *"most people can't do that,"* or that constant warning against trying something new because it is *"too risky?"*

Also, think about when you are constantly hearing negative judgments regarding other people. Exposure to this negativity can have a major impact on your overall sense of positivity, and **lead you to become negative yourself.**

They are a source of constant complaints.

A complaint refers to a circumstance in one's life that they wish were different. This could be something small, like a misplaced set of keys, or something bigger, like being mistreated by a boss.

Even if a complaint is justified, it still means that we are not getting our way. Negative people often feel like they are never getting their way, so they have a lot of things to complain about.

They cannot see that their complaining is adding to their dissatisfaction with life.

They think everyone else is wrong. They are the only people who are ever right.

Seriously, how can everyone else be so stupid all the time? Between co-workers, clients, and even friends, negative people often feel like the only intelligent people on earth.

What they don't see is that if everyone around them is always wrong and they can hardly handle it, the problem likely lies within them.

People are smart—not everyone, but a good amount of them. Negative people don't realize that they are not the smartest people in the world.

They love to dwell on bad news.

Negative people love approaching others and mentioning the most recent terrible news. The problem here is that overexposure to negative news affects a person more deeply than was previously thought

Alternatively, if you are constantly around positive people, you are more likely to feel positive about the world and the people around you.

If you want to increase your overall life satisfaction, then it is in your best interest to learn how to handle the negative people in your life

But what's the deal with negative people and how their psychology works? Most importantly, are they really bad for you? Can their negativity rub off on you and become your default operational mode as well?

Why are some people so negative?

Whiners and complainers keep nagging because they feel helpless. Not to say that negativity is a mental disorder, but many psychological problems develop because of the feeling of lack of control accompanied by an overwhelming desire to control at least something. Negative people feel weak and powerless over their environment and the outcomes of their lives. To make things worse, they are unable to change their attitude or <u>the way they feel about things</u>. There are several factors that play role in this:

> ➤ natural disposition,
> ➤ past negative experiences that formed a negative filter that messes with one's perception of things and events,
> ➤ health situations, such as hormonal imbalance and inadequate levels of brain chemicals.

Many happier and more proactive people make the mistake of thinking that every time somebody complains about something, they must be asking for their advice. They feel particularly frustrated that their every suggestion is met with "Yes, but...", and then discarded as something that won't work.

What we all need to understand is that most of the time, pessimists nag and complain only to vent and validate their feelings. Talking about their problems gives them temporary relief; they simply need an outlet to vent their frustration. However, it's important to understand that they are not asking for your advice, nor do they get particularly happy when you suggest something. Yes, it must be hard to wrap your mind around this if you are an optimistic go-getter, which only proves that you two are very different people.

Not all pessimists complain

Not all negative people become annoying naggers. Some quietly suffer from their negativity and deal with its consequences on their own. Unfortunately, their world is even darker, and they are very prone to depression. In that sense, they deserve our compassion.

Is being around negative people bad for you?

Venting is a part of human relationships. From time to time, we need an ear, a shoulder to cry on. We rant for a while, sometimes for a long while, and then we move on. Not everything has to be "fixed", and simply listening to a person is one of the greatest gifts you can give. However, some people take simple venting to a whole new level, and here is when it becomes dangerous for you as well. Here are some of the tell-tell signs of a toxic person:

> **They rarely talk about anything positive;** all they do is whine, whine and whine. Usually, they will be focusing on just one main topic: their boss, their family member or a particular person they hate but are forced to deal with. Occasionally it might not involve relationships, such as health or money issues.

> **They are completely uninterested in you.** Try telling them something about your life and you will have your answer. If the person is toxic, they will likely interrupt you after a couple of minutes and take the stage again.

> **You are not allowed to disagree with them.** To them, your duty is to listen and support. You are not allowed

to express other opinions or politely disagree. If you aren't with them, you are against them. What they do here is they are building a coalition, and if you aren't sharing their views completely, you cannot be considered their friend. If they can find someone who listens and supports you "better" than you, they will be out of your life in a snap.

> **They are narcissists.** Narcissists are particularly prone to toxic venting but not every person who gets carried away is necessarily a narcissist. However, if the person you are dealing with has <u>narcissistic tendencies</u>, the relationship may be even more unhealthy for you.

Even when presented with good news, negative people find some way to look at it negatively.

Perhaps you are excited to share the news that you landed your dream job, which includes a huge raise. Their reaction? *"That's good, but your taxes will be higher."*

Negative people can always find a way to make positive events sound negative. They will warn you to be careful, caution you of any possible obstacles, and tell you to think about it before acting on anything.

Can you think of some of the negative people in your life? Why do you think they are so negative? Is it their job, relationship, or schooling?

Think about this, and be aware of their emotions and behaviour when you are around them. Then, think about your own emotions when you are with them. Do you feel tired? Do you start feeling a bit negative yourself? If so, it is important to remember that it is not you, it is them.

Ways to deal with negative people

Being around negative people may affect your attitude. If avoiding them is simply not an option, try the following:

1- Set boundaries.

Don't feel pressured to listen to a negative person and don't spend time with them than you need to.

It is important to realize what you are willing or able to tolerate when it comes to negativity. You are not required to listen to everything a negative person has to say.

You certainly have the right to get up and walk away or focus your attention elsewhere. Remember that their negativity will impact your thoughts and feelings, and affect your attitude.

For example, say you are doing a project at work that you are enjoying. Unfortunately, a co-worker who is also working on the project continues to complain about it.

This could alter your experience with the project, and you could start to dislike it as well. This is why it is important to limit your exposure to negativity.

Instead, surround yourself with people who share your positive feelings. If you have a friend who tends to be negative, you don't have to necessarily never see them again — but it is best to be aware of yourself and your feelings so you can pick and choose when to interact with that person

For example, if you are going through a tough time, you likely don't want to add to that by being around someone negative. But, if you are feeling pretty confident in your life at the moment, it may be a good time to visit with that person.

Just be aware that you will want to limit your exposure to your positive attitude does not become negatively impacted.

You have the right to set boundaries and limit your exposure to toxicity. If your negative friend is demanding your time, or if you have a negative co-worker that you can't avoid, tell them your boundaries.

This may feel awkward, or even sound hurtful to the other person, but you deserve happiness, and it will be worth it in the long run.

2- Don't make their problems your problems.

It will most certainly bring you down if you focus too much of your time on your negative friend's problems. Practice self-awareness so you can gauge when your thoughts are beginning to decline and your life is starting to be affected.

You don't have a responsibility for other people's feelings or actions, but you are responsible for yourself. For this reason, at some point, you need to put your well-being ahead of others and focus on your own life rather than theirs.

This is not something that you should feel guilty about doing. You likely want to feel like you are an empathetic healer, and the truth is, empathy is a great thing to have.

But don't let your empathy for other people become so much of a burden that you are no longer able to feel empathetic towards other people in your life. Don't guilt yourself for putting yourself first.

You have to recognize and understand that everyone is on a unique journey in life. If you have a friend who always has some kind of drama going on, let that be their journey.

Don't make it your own. Don't allow yourself to get pulled into their drama and have it impact your positive journey through life.

3- Help some people deal with their negativity.

There may be some people in your life who are very important to you, and therefore you want to help them deal with their negative thoughts.

This probably won't be true for someone who is temporarily passing through your life, but if you have a family member or a close friend who seems like they could use some help, you have options. Someone may even ask you for help. So it is best to be equipped with some strategies.

First, you can show them kindness. Do something nice for them that they really can't put a negative spin on. Maybe buy them their favourite candy, or surprise them one day with a nice card. Give them a hug when you see them. Do anything to make them feel like you care.

It is also helpful to lend them a smile when you see them. Smiles can be as contagious as negativity, and you can pass on your compassion by showing you are happy when you are with a negative person. You never know—your positivity could rub off on them.

Give your negative friends compliments and positive reinforcement so they feel validated. This may help them look on the brighter side of things instead of continuing to focus on things that have gone wrong.

Try to give a compliment that isn't common or superficial. For example, rather than saying "I like your shirt," say something like, "I was impressed with how you handled XYZ this week. Your communication skills are something to be proud of."

If you show respect and encouragement, you will be more likely to receive it in return. Additionally, if you can think of a solution to their problems, go ahead and suggest it. Put yourself in their shoes, and think about what you would do if you were in their situation, no matter how insignificant the problem may seem to you.

Use your active listening skills to allow your friend to tell you exactly what is going on, and make a suggestion about how the issue can be resolved, or even how they can try to move on.

Doing this can help them overcome their negativity, which would be beneficial to them in so many aspects of their life. If you are successful in this, then you can be proud that you have had a positive influence on someone else's life.

But remember that in the end, their attitude isn't your responsibility, so if you are unable to change it, you have to accept that and move on with your own life.

4- Don't rationalize.

Negative feelings are often irrational and trying to analyse and explain a negative person's behaviour might not be the best thing you could do with your time and mental energy. Do not become emotionally invested in their issues.

5- Look for positive influence.

Try to get closer to more positive people, read positive books and practice finding solutions. Listen to positive, motivational podcasts, or find some YouTube videos that send positive messages to the viewers. Doing this can also help you learn how to meditate, as there are many meditation podcasts you can listen to find one that suits you the best.

6- Create a positive environment in your personal life.

The environment you surround yourself with will influence your mood. Whether you are at home or work, creating a positive environment and having positive energies can make your life much better and healthier.

To do this, start by surrounding yourself with people who share your attitude of positivity. You will feed off of each other, and contribute even more to each other's positive attitudes.

You have to put forth the work to create the environment that you want in your life. You can do this by spreading your happiness and going out of your way to lift those around you. Also, practice gratitude—not only outwardly, but also internally.

Be conscious of the things in your life that you are thankful for, and be sure to tell someone if you are grateful for something they did. You can also encourage positive thinking from others by showing off your positivity

Living with a negative person

Sometimes it's not easy to avoid negative people, especially when they live in your home. It could be your partner, your sibling, your parent or even one of your adult children. Here are some steps you can take to preserve your well-being and stay optimistic while living with a negative person:

- ➢ **Focus on yourself.** Do what you need to do to stay positive and move in the right direction.

- ➢ **Don't overanalyse.** Once again, negativity is often irrational and trying to explain their feelings may drag you down.

- ➢ **Be a positive influence.** Focus on staying positive no matter what and show them a good example they can follow.

- ➢ **Avoid arguments.** It's easy to accuse your partner or family member of excessive negativity, but arguing in itself is not a positive thing to do; just lead by example instead.

They never look for the good in the world. Albert Einstein reportedly once said,

"There are two ways to live your life. One is as though nothing is a miracle. The other is as though everything is a miracle."

Start by identifying the biggest sources of negativity in your life, finding out if you have a toxic personality, and making a commitment to change the dynamics of your interaction with these people. Set some boundaries and limit your exposure to them, even if it means telling them that those are your intentions.

➔ **"Nobody can hurt me without my permission"- Mahatma Gandhi**

One of the purest and most beautiful acts of kindness is when someone shares their smile because they see somebody else without one. It's those small things that speak volumes about someone's intentions to make the world a better place.

Not everyone is going to get you, accept you, or even try to understand you. Some people will receive your energy well. Make peace with that and keep moving towards your joy.

<u>I promise my friend you'll quickly find that taking this proactive approach can transform your levels of happiness and decrease the amount of stress in your life.</u>

Chapter – 05
Self-Love

Byron Katie said, "Do you want to meet the love of your life? Look in the mirror."

According to the Brain and Behaviour Research Foundation, "Self-love is a state of appreciation for oneself that grows from actions that support our physical, psychological and spiritual growth. Self-love means having a high regard for your well-being and happiness. Self-love means taking care of your own needs and not sacrificing your well-being to please others. Self-love means not settling for less than you deserve." Not a small task!

Here is how that looked on my journey. I focused on creating what I wanted in my life, rather than what I thought others wanted me to do or be. I decided to only be with people that treated me with love and respect. I deepened my spiritual practices.

I allowed myself to do things that bring me joy. Some things were simple… turquoise nail polish on my toes; hiking at any speed I felt like. Other steps took a bit of commitment, such as letting go of some habits that did not serve me.

Let's take a look at the elements of self-love.

Self-love It sounds great, but what does it actually mean? How do we love ourselves and why does it matter?

Self-compassion is a way of relating to yourself that does not involve harshly judging or punishing yourself for every mistake you make. Self-love means that you accept yourself fully, treat yourself with kindness and respect, and nurture your growth and well-being.

Self-love encompasses not only how you treat yourself but also your thoughts and feelings about yourself. So, when you conceptualize self-love, you can try to imagine what you would do for yourself, how you had to talk to yourself, and how you had to feel about yourself that reflects love and concern.

When you love yourself, you have an overall positive view of yourself. This doesn't mean you feel positive about yourself all the time. That would be unrealistic! For example, I can temporarily feel upset, angry, or disappointed with myself and still love myself. If this is confusing, think about how this works in other relationships. I can love my son even though I sometimes feel angry or disappointed with him. Even amid my anger and disappointment, my love for him informs how I relate to him. It allows me to forgive him, consider his feelings, meet his needs, and make decisions that will support his well-being. Self-love is very much the same. This means, if you know how to love others, you know how to love yourself!

Your Best Friend Is You

Begin by treating yourself like you would a good friend you love and respect. Each day, look in the mirror and appreciate yourself for something. Did you work out? Keep a promise to yourself or someone else? Create something or learn something? Tell yourself, "Good job!" Or appreciate some qualities you have, such as being friendly, considerate, or capable.

What if you feel down? Tell yourself you can see you are feeling low and that you understand. Ask yourself what you need. Tell yourself that you love yourself no matter what. Hug yourself or something soft that comforts you.

Doing this is not narcissistic or selfish. It is allowing you to fully participate in and contribute to life.

Can you see how this is a giant first step in bringing more love into your life? How can someone love you when you are not loving yourself?

Benefits of Self-Love

Although the phrase "self-love" is not generally used in psychology research, the idea of self-love is often thought to be a crucial aspect of well-being. Some regard having positive feelings about the self as "the key to happiness, success, and popularity". More specifically, self-esteem contributes to positive feelings and greater initiative. Even in our well-being survey, we see that self-love is the factor most closely linked to happiness.

Why do we need to love ourselves?

If you grew up without any models for self-love or anyone who talked to you about the importance of being good to yourself, you might question its value.

Well, without self-love, you're likely to be highly self-critical and fall into people-pleasing and perfectionism. You're more likely to tolerate abuse or mistreatment from others. You may neglect your own needs and feelings because you don't value yourself. And you may self-sabotage or make decisions that aren't in your own best interest.

Self-love is the foundation that allows us to be assertive, set boundaries and create healthy relationships with others, practice self-care, pursue our interests and goals, and feel proud of who we are.

Sometimes if we're feeling bad about ourselves, it can be hard to even think of how to be self-loving. We're often speaking to ourselves with an air of negativity and we need some self-loving affirmations to help us learn how to speak to ourselves more kindly. Here are some examples that may be useful. Try using these examples to be more loving toward yourself.

Love your personality

> Maybe you are kind, funny, interesting, brave, strong, or have other personality traits that you love. Try focusing on these more than your less desirable traits to grow your self-love.

Love your skills

> What are you good at? Maybe you can fix a car, draw, run, communicate, problem-solve, or do something else well. We all have skills that are worth loving if we pay attention to them.

Love your appearance

> I know, I know. Many of us have problems with the way we look. We compare ourselves to models and actors and can end up feeling like we can't compete. But that's not a fair comparison. So what *part* of your

appearance do you love? Do you have nice eyes, ears, eyebrows, or toes? Make note of these parts of you that are easier to love.

Self-Love Affirmations

Once we have identified some parts of ourselves that we believe are worthy of self-love, it may be helpful to create some affirmations or statements we repeat to ourselves to remind us that we are worthy of self-love. For example, let's say you've been going through a tough time. You might create the affirmation, "I'm strong, capable, and worthy." Or, if we're struggling after a breakup, maybe we write an affirmation that says, "I am kind, loving, and deserving of love."

Whatever affirmation we write; we just need to make sure it makes us feel good about ourselves. If it doesn't fit you, or your situation, or doesn't feel authentic, then it's not likely to help so much.

Permit Yourself to Love Your Body

Your body is a gorgeous and fantastic tool for exploration. Your body wasn't made only to be aesthetically pleasing to the rest of the world. It's not an elaborate vase. It is a tool that enables you to accomplish all of your life's goals.

Climb, eat, go places, go to work, knit… as if it were your child, take care of your body. With nothing but love and the knowledge that everything is ideal just the way it is. Loving yourself and falling head over heels for your appearance is what self-love is all about!

We are instructed that achieving the ideal body will make us happy. You are familiar with that kind; it is an unattainable beauty standard frequently airbrushed over.

No matter how much weight you lose, how many goods you purchase, or how much plastic surgery you have. A body cannot contain happiness because there is nowhere for it to reside.

Happiness results from accepting oneself. Realize that having a body is what you need to feel secure, successful, and like you can do anything you want.

You can do whatever you want regardless of how your body is shaped, so stop spending time attempting to follow a particular diet type and instead get Happiness. It is found within.

Self-Love Tips

If we're struggling when we try to think of how to speak to ourselves lovingly, here are some tips that can inspire self-love.

1. Forgive yourself
2. Be compassionate with yourself
3. Let go
4. Take your power back
5. Meditate on self-love
6. Practice gratitude
7. Be loving towards others

How to Practice Self-Love?

These self-love tips are all well and good, but how do you practice them? Here's some more guidance.

Forgive yourself

When we hold onto anger towards others, it ends up hurting us the most. One study showed that adults who completed a six-week forgiveness training reported lower stress, anger, and hurt than people who didn't undergo the training (Harris, et al., 2006). They also felt more capable of forgiving and had greater optimism immediately after the training and four months later. This suggests that working through resentment and finding ways to forgive is good for well-being.

Be self-compassionate

Self-compassion is when we are kind and caring towards ourselves. Rather than judging and criticizing ourselves, we show ourselves the compassion we might show someone else. Perhaps we do this by giving ourselves a break when we're working too hard. Or maybe, we do so by writing ourselves a kind letter, saying the things we wish someone else would say to us. Whatever our method, practising self-compassion is a great way to grow self-love.

Let go

When we hold onto negativity or let our rumination get the best of us, we can get stuck in negative thoughts that keep us down. We might feel bad about something we said to someone or be regretful about the way we acted. But focusing on these past events isn't helpful. Instead, we need to try to let go and focus on the present moment. By doing so, it can be easier to find self-love.

Embrace the Fact That You Can't Control Everything

The only things you can control are the ones you can change, including your reactions. Recognize that, like the weather, you do not influence other people, their decisions, or their actions.

Instead of attempting to control everything in life, focus on how you respond to it. Do the best you can and then put your hands up and say, "It is in the hands of the Gods now," letting everything work itself out rather than attempting to control everyone and everything. Everything finally resolves itself.

Take your power back

A lack of autonomy or control over our own lives is often what makes us feel bad about ourselves. But the truth is we give a lot of our power away. Sure, maybe we have a job we don't like and a boss that micromanages us. But if we can find ways to demonstrate our skills outside of work, perhaps even eventually switching jobs, this can help us gain a sense of control and power. So try looking for things you do have control over and taking action when you can.

Try self-love meditations

Guided meditations can help shift our thoughts in ways that help us focus on new things. By trying a self-love meditation, we are guided to think about the ways we are good, valuable, worthwhile people with a lot to offer. Here's a guided self-love meditation to try:

Music for un-guided self-love meditation

Practice gratitude

I always say this, although gratitude for others and things in our lives is a great practice for boosting well-being, we can also practice gratitude for ourselves. For example, we might tell ourselves "thanks" for the good work we are doing or for eating healthy meals yesterday. Or, we might give ourselves heartfelt gratitude for "staying strong and not giving into to our co-workers' unreasonable demands", or for "allowing ourselves to take a nap when we were exhausted." By learning how to communicate with ourselves in grateful ways we can extend the benefits of gratitude in ways that may help us boost self-love.

Be loving towards others

Love is a skill. It takes practice to both give and receive love. If we didn't receive enough love or witness love being given when we were young, we may not have adequately learned how to give and receive love. It's okay though because it's a skill and it takes practice for us all. If we practice being loving towards others and ourselves, we'll grow this skill and it'll get easier over time.

Remember Who You Are

You have endured a lot, yet you have overcome it, growing stronger with each experience. Please keep in mind who you are.

You should welcome adversity because it will make life more fascinating and help you go where you want. Experiencing feelings like self-doubt is natural, but don't let it overconsume your thoughts.

Stop Being Too Tough on Yourself

Not everything you think is true. We all have a critic who wants to keep us tiny and secure. The drawback is that it prevents us from living complete lives. One of the biggest things that might prevent someone from loving themselves is being hard on themselves.

You can improve your relationship by learning to love yourself and practising self-love. This is essential if you want to develop a strong connection with other people. Although it takes time to develop self-love, you will undoubtedly get better at it.

Even if you're under stress, consider all that you've already accomplished. You will be one step closer to being the best version once you discover how to be kind to yourself.

Have a wonderful time! Get out there and pursue the activities that ignite your passion. Enjoy them, enjoy who you are, and take in your amazing life.

Chapter – 06
Frame of mind

(Attitude)

The greatest discovery of my generation is that human beings can alter their lives by altering their attitudes of mind- William James.

Attitude is everything:

My dad used to say those words to me when I was a sore loser after losing in a game while playing. Fortunately, I have a friendly, great and supportive father **(Mr Ismail),** I remember one story which made to look for positivity in any situation, my mom and dad are the best teachers in my life. In my childhood when I was 9 years old my dad taught me, how to play chess game and he is one of the masterminds in Chess game, I learnt all the tricks and rules of the game while playing with him, and even I have started liking the game cause it's pretty much interested and tricky game to use your intelligence. Competitively I started playing with my dad, but I lost all the games whenever I used to play, but whenever I used to Sit and play the game, hoping that I will win, I end up disappointed whenever I lose the game. You don't believe me that I lost 1000s of the games with my dad. But I used to get a lot of anger and I decided that I can't win over my dad. I used to get angry thinking that I am one loser and started feeling negative about myself and towards the game.

But my dad silently observed my all behaviours and started motivating me that I can also play well and win the game, but I have decided and made room in my mind that I will never win against my dad on this damn chess board. Several times my dad asked me to let's play the game and I used to refuse with a negative mindset.

One day I was just studying over the table and my dad was telling to my sisters that if anybody wins against me. The winner is going to an ice cream or whatever they wish to have. And hearing that my eyes went bigger and bigger, I felt happy in case I win over my dad and I might get ice cream. But negative thoughts already occupied my mind. Fear inside me that was telling me that I can't win over my dad. My dad said will you give it a try? He came up to me and said you can do it this time I can see hunger and anger in you my son. Come let's play, I was not in the mood to play but, I got little positive hope and wanted to play.

Eventually, we started playing the game with so much intensity and seriousness, and my dad had already studied my negative behaviours, that he started losing in front of me and he observed that I started getting happy and confident about the game. Finally, I win the game and I could say it was my first win against my dad, it was emotional and he said to me, "Don't ever try to hang up your mind with a negative attitude and have faith in yourself. The moment you take in a sportive and positive attitude way I'm sure my son you stand as a champion one day." That made me realise positive attitude is everything in life. As I got older and wiser, as most of us do, I started to realize that my dad was right about that fact. And, I also started to realize that lessons applied to more than just sports or activities in my life.

What is attitude?

Attitude is **the way you look at life**. It is the way you choose to see and respond to events, situations, people, and yourself. Your attitude is not something that happens to you. You choose your attitude. Your attitude is created by your thoughts, and you choose your thoughts.

You are the architect of your **frame of mind.** You decide how you will perceive and process the events of life and work. You decide if your mindset is positive or negative. If you want to feel better, you have to think better. To be positive in the way you feel, it is necessary to be disciplined in the way you think.

The performance begins within you. Your mind has enormous power. Indeed, your mind is your most important performance resource. How you see and respond to the events of life and work is shaped by **your mindset and patterns of thinking**. Therefore, an essential key to success is to train your mind and use it wisely.

Attitude is everything! It shifts your perspective to your circumstances which in turn affects how you view your own life.

What is your attitude to life?

Most people are in the habit of complaining. Some people complain they don't have enough money to pursue their dreams. Others claim where they were born or grew up limited their chances of achieving their dreams. Still, others are more focused on being jealous of the success of others, isn't it?

Mate, you should be thinking about how you can take charge and be in control of your life rather than let the circumstances dictate your life. It's time you stopped complaining and started taking action towards achieving what you always complain you don't have this or that bla, bla, blaa etc... It's time you picked yourself up and started fighting for your dreams, rather than feeling sorry for yourself.

The difference between winners and losers is their **attitude to life**. Winners are optimists and losers are pessimists; **Winners see the glass as half full while losers see it as half empty**. Nobody has it all. So, I want you to change your attitude and start seeing life from a very positive perspective rather than have a negative outlook on life. You're what you see. Achievers have always had a positive outlook on life and **you have the power to spin a positive story over your own life**.

Why Your Attitude is so Important?

"Control the controllable" – that's a statement that makes every control freak shutter with disdain. At its core, what it's saying is that we need to focus our energy on controlling the things we can control in some way, shape, or form, and not fret about those things that are out of our control. And if we're being completely honest, there aren't many things that we can control in life. But, one of the few things that we can always control is our attitude. And it's vitally important that we do so. **The reason why is that your attitude influences your actions. And we all know that it's our actions that determine our success.**

As the saying goes, **"Your attitude determines your altitude."** Meaning that the type of attitude you approach life with will significantly impact the level of success you will or will not have. Typically, when someone has a bad attitude, it negatively affects their action. These are the naysayers, doubters, and negative Nancies of the world. I don't know many of those types of people who are out there just killing it. Those tend to be the people who, because of their frustration from a lack of results and success in their own lives, troll and try to tear down those who are trying to create success in theirs.

On the other hand, when you have a positive attitude and outlook, you're much more likely to take action and get things done. And, not only that, having a positive attitude makes you much more likely to be supportive of others and helpful to them in whatever it is that they have going on. So, an added benefit of a positive attitude is that you're able to foster better relationships. I don't know of many millionaires or billionaires that walk around with bad attitudes. It's usually quite the opposite. They tend to have great attitudes and outlooks in life, which has allowed them to create the success they've achieved.

What is a Negative Attitude?

A negative attitude is the result of negative thinking. It is a lack of mental discipline. It focuses on the problem and stops looking for solutions or opportunities. A negative attitude can only survive on a steady diet of negative thinking and negative self-talk. A negative attitude is habit-forming, and it has an impact on you and the people around you. A negative attitude affects you physically. A person with a negative attitude will almost always lose to a person with a positive attitude. Sadly, many people with a negative attitude are stuck in a doom loop because they have a negative attitude about improving their attitude. This is not a good place to be!

What is a Positive Attitude?

A positive attitude is the result of a disciplined and deliberate way of seeing, thinking, and responding to life. It is a mental discipline. It is intentional. It is mental toughness. A positive attitude is not naïve, and it does not sugar-coat problems. Rather, it sees and acknowledges problems and then focuses on finding solutions and opportunities. It looks for the opportunity within the problem. A positive attitude is habit-forming, and it has an impact on you and the people around you. A positive attitude affects you physically. A person with a positive attitude will almost always outperform a person with a negative attitude.

Now that we know why your attitude is so important, let's look at a few must-have attitudes that you need in your life.

Disciplined Thinking

To have a positive and proactive attitude, you must be disciplined and deliberate about the way you see and think about events, situations, people, and yourself. The way you think drives the way you feel; therefore, consciously managing the way you perceive and process events is essential to a positive attitude.

A key element of mental discipline is paying attention to and managing your self-talk. Self-talk is what you say to yourself about situations you're facing. It is how you choose to interpret and explain the events you are experiencing.

Managing your self-talk is critical because words carry thoughts, and thoughts create feelings.

Here's how it works: Your attitude begins with what you choose to focus on and the words you use to express your focus. A person with a default-driven, negative mindset will focus on a situation and say something like, **"That's a rubbish idea. It will never work out."**

A person with a discipline-driven, positive mindset will look at the same situation and say something like, **"That's an idea. I'm not sure if it will work, but let's explore it further and find out a solution." Note carefully** the difference in language between these two mindsets.

The default way of thinking uses phrases like "never" and "always." The disciplined way of thinking uses language like "possible" "maybe" and "explore." Because attitude is so immediately responsive to language, the negative words will trigger negative feelings, and the positive words will trigger positive feelings.

Manage Your Focus

Understand one thing that **"The way you think drives the way you feel".** When faced with a difficult or frustrating situation, you can choose to focus on the problem, engage in negative self-talk, and focus your emotional energy on worrying and complaining; or you can acknowledge what is challenging, discipline yourself to see the big picture, engage in productive self-talk, and focus your emotional energy on finding a solution or on enduring the challenge.

Make a note mate **(this is important)** that a positive attitude does not ignore problems. It does not gloss over hard issues or disregard what is challenging.

A positive attitude sees the situation more accurately and thoroughly because it does not lock in on the negative aspects of the situation.

A negative attitude tends to be narrow, limiting, and rigid. Once a negative attitude finds what it is looking for (which it almost always does), it stops looking and stops thinking. A positive attitude, on the other hand, tends to give greater perspective and insight because it stays fully engaged in the search for a solution.

Attitude changes everything – it can change your life

"It's your reaction to adversity, not the adversity itself that determines how your life's story will develop."-Dieter F. Uchtdorf

The attitude you approach anything with is entirely your choice. The way you choose to respond mirrors your attitude and so by changing your attitude you can change your perspective and change your life. Your attitude reflects the way you see the world and how you live in it. It affects every aspect of your life, your happiness, relationships, health, well-being and success. Developing a positive attitude that you apply with action can change the way you live your life regardless of the challenges or adversity you face. In this post, I want to share with you some of the ways attitude can change the way you live your life.

Must have attitudes in life

Attitude of Positivity

Positivity has a direct relationship with possibilities. Negative people tend to have a fixed mindset and are closed off to all of the possibility that exists in life. Negativity and a victim's mindset go hand in hand. Conversely, when someone has a positive outlook and attitude, they are much more likely to have a mindset and are open to the abundance that exists within the world.

As I mentioned above, whether you have a positive attitude or not, will affect the action you take. When we take action and achieve a desired outcome, we further expand our minds to possibilities, which furthers our positivity. And you'll see why, in just a moment, having a positive attitude is necessary for you to be able to have the other attitudes we're going to discuss below.

Practice gratitude.

Achieving an **"attitude of gratitude"** entails more than simply recognising what's wonderful in your own life. Take action by thanking other people for their gifts or kindness to you, even if that gift is something as simple as a smile or an acknowledgement. Don't take yourself too seriously. If you want to be happier nurture the ability to laugh at yourself. It will help to balance your drive and purpose with **a dash of gentle humour and fun**.

an attitude of gratitude is so important. It takes you out of focusing on what you don't have **(i.e. being stuck in comparison mode and having a negative attitude)** and helps you to focus on all that you do have.

When we think about life from an energetic perspective, there's nothing that raises our vibration more than gratitude. Focusing on consciously adding more gratitude into your life will be one of the most transformative things you will do, and will positively impact all areas of your life.

The attitude of Greatness.

One of the things about having a good attitude is that it's a matter of choice – you have to choose to have a good attitude. Because of the need to survive experienced by our ancestors, our minds naturally have a bent towards the negative. It was a survival mechanism.

Another thing that is a choice in life, and something that will positively impact your life, is becoming great at something. If you take a step back and look at the relationship between a positive attitude and becoming great at something, you'll see that it's a symbiotic, two-way relationship. Becoming great at something will give you a **boost in confidence**, which will positively impact your attitude. Looking at it the other way, it typically takes having a positive attitude to want to become great at something.

One key thing to add here is that you need to make sure that you're pursuing greatness at something that you enjoy and that fulfils you. Otherwise, you won't get that two-way benefit we just discussed. I always did well in school, but I didn't enjoy it much, so I didn't go into it with a great attitude.

Think of any great sportsman – they aren't walking around with a bad attitude. They may have a chip on their shoulder, and be hyper-competitive, but they tend to be positive people. And that positivity opens them up to possibility, which deepens their drive to be great. As they continue to pursue greatness, they become more confident, which partner fuels their beliefs about possibilities. And the cycle continues. So, if you're struggling with a bad attitude, seek to become great at something and see if that doesn't change.

The attitude you choose will determine the outcome

Select the most useful attitude that will help you with the challenges you face. The attitude you choose will determine how successfully you will manage the challenge or situation.

Consider how that attitude will determine what you say, your behaviour and action and what will be the outcome.

Always take action with a purpose

Before you take any action, decide how it will serve your greater goals. Act with thought and consideration when choosing an attitude that will help you take the actions that will manage the challenges you face.

Step out of your comfort zone to the Growth zone.

If you stay stuck in your comfort zone, it may seem safe and familiar but if you don't challenge yourself nothing will ever change. **If you don't stretch yourself every day**, you will never find out what you are truly capable of. Have a get up to go, take a risk and transition from your **comfort zone** into your **growth zone** where you will gain purpose, live your dreams, set goals and overcome the obstacles that have been holding you back.

Take action without expecting success

Change happens and confidence grows from taking action. It's where you learn most about yourself and build resilience. Of course, you have to make decisions and plan your actions to achieve the results you want, but it's a big mistake to expect those damn results and then be upset or downhearted when you don't get them. Take the best action you can but don't fixate on the result.

Use setbacks or disappointments to learn from and build resilience

Rather than feeling bad if you fail, reflect on your actions and see what you can do to better or learn what to do next. I underline this or take a note **Growth comes from failing and learning, again and again.** Seek out those who share your positive attitude. It's a known fact that your brain automatically copies the behaviours of the people around you. Therefore, it makes sense to surround yourself with people who have a positive and proactive attitude and move away from those who are unduly negative or drain your energy.

Take responsibility.

Taking responsibility for your attitude is the first step. **If you can say, "The attitude I possess is my responsibility and no one else's"** you're well on your way to changing your mindset. Blaming your attitude on other people or other things won't improve anything.

Develop good habits.

Negative thoughts lead to negative beliefs; negative beliefs can become the basis for wrong decisions that lead to wrong actions. When this cycle is repeated, it feeds a bad attitude. Instead, try developing one good habit at a time, such as getting up earlier or exercising. Breaking the cycle with one good habit can lead to developing more good habits—and a more positive outlook.

Find other positive people.

Avoid time with negative people; all they do is bring you down to their level and slap you with their idiocy. Find people who have a can-do attitude and who bring out the best in you and others too.

Look for Mentors.

Look for mentors. Look for those that have already achieved what you're trying to achieve and learn from them.

When you do all these and start having the right attitude to life, you'll have access to all the beautiful things of life you have always wanted my friend.

STORIES OF SETBACKS AND GETTING SUCCESS.

It's human nature to oversimplify the success of the people we admire. From the outside looking in, it's easy to make judgments about how certain people got to where they are.

It's easy to chalk up the success of others to a "good upbringing" or a "right place, right time", but in most cases, we have no idea what we're talking about.

we're going to be looking at the true motivational stories behind some of the world's most successful people. These inspirational stories will give you a glimpse into the challenges that forged these high-achievers into people that we admire.

Peeling back the layers behind the facade of successful people can give us insight into how to handle setbacks in our own lives. Not only that, but they serve as a wakeup call by defining what it takes to achieve our own goals and dreams

Let's dive into some true motivational stories behind successful people that will I hope will be eye-opening for you to read about.

In each of these stories, you're going to notice a common theme – failure.

Many of these inspirational people that we're about to cover failed over and over again to get to where they are now.

They experienced things that may have made other people throw in the towel. But because they didn't let their failures define them, they were able to see their goals through and live purposeful lives.

Read these true motivational stories closely. With each experience, think to yourself – would this have stopped me?

Story – 01

Steve Jobs Was laid off from The Company He Started

To start this list of true motivational stories, it's only right to start with the late, great Steve Jobs.

We all know Steve Jobs as the marketing genius and co-founder of Apple, one of the most successful companies in the world today.

Contrary to many people on this list, Jobs was a fairly quick succession. By the age of 25, his net worth was over $100 million.

What you probably don't know is that he was fired from Apple, the company he co-founded, by a man named John Sculley. Ironically, just a few years earlier Jobs had hired Scully to help run the company.

Jobs wanted the CEO title, but the board felt like he was too young and too difficult to work with, so they ousted him.

How would you feel if you were fired right in your prime from the very company that you built from the ground up? Jobs was humiliated, but he didn't see this situation as permanent – **just a temporary setback.**

Almost immediately after getting fired from Apple, he founded a company called NeXT. He poured all of his efforts into building an operating system that would change the world, and he succeeded.

Realizing the value of what Jobs was doing at NeXT, Apple ended up buying them for $429 million. A few months later, Jobs was named interim CEO and then eventually acquired the coveted CEO title that he had gotten fired for aiming at 12 years prior.

After the biggest failure of his career, all it took was twelve years of struggle and work to reach his ultimate goal.

Would you have the patience to wait it out?

Story – 02

Walt Disney Had to Survive on Dogfood

Continuing with this list of true motivational stories about success, we have Walt Disney.

Many of you know Waly Disney today as the legendary animation magnate who is responsible for creating some of the most iconic cartoon characters ever – Mickey Mouse, Cinderella, Donald Duck, and more.

What you probably didn't know about is the rocky road that led to his success

Walt Disney was the fourth son born among his five siblings. His father Elias reportedly abused each of his children and was a dominating figure in their lives.

To find solace from the trouble in his house, he began to take up drawing. He watched as each of his siblings decided one by one to run away from their father and start new lives.

Eventually, he decided to follow suit and lied about his age to become an ambulance driver during World War 1.

After returning home from the war, Disney maintained his love of art and landed an apprenticeship at a commercial art studio in Kansas City. Feeling like he was destined for bigger things, he decided to leave and start his own cartoon company with his brother Roy.

After a couple of years, the company went bankrupt. Disney was flat-broke, so to save money he survived on dog food just to keep his expenses low.

With just $40 to his name, he packed up and moved to Los Angeles to pursue an acting career, but that failed too.

Eventually, Disney finally got his big break by creating a successful cartoon character named Oswald The Rabbit. Yet, failure and disappointment were still lurking around the corner.

When he got back to New York to renegotiate his contract, he discovered that his producer had stolen his team of animators out from under him. More importantly, though, he no longer had any legal rights to the character he created.

Noticing a common theme here? Failure. Failure. And more failure.

Time and time again, it appeared as if Disney's dreams were never going to amount to anything. He experienced repeated setbacks that would've taken most people out of the game completely.

It was on the ride home from New York that he created Mickey Mouse.

To turn this giant mouse into what he thought it could be, he needed financial backing. And over 300 bankers laughed him out of their offices when he presented the idea of Mickey Mouse.

Yep, that's right. One of the most iconic cartoon characters ever was rejected 300 times before someone finally bought into Disney's vision.

You thought J.k. Rowling's story of rejection was bad? Multiply that by 30 and that's how much harder Disney had to work to bring his idea to life.

And as they say, the rest is history. 26 Academy Awards and $130 billion later, Disney has left a legacy in the film industry that cannot be denied.

From eating dog food and being rejected over 300 times, to being hailed as one of the greatest visionaries of all time.

Setback after setback. Defeat after defeat. Disney persevered because he had a vision that was strong enough to overcome all of it.

Story – 03

Thomas Edison's 10,000 Ways That Didn't Work

Most of you know this story already, but it's worth mentioning because it's an exemplary story of how important an ingredient failure is to creating success.

Thomas Edison was born to be an inventor. In 1877, he invented the carbon transmitter – a device responsible for cleaning up the audio on the other side of the telephone. That same year, he invented the phonograph, which was able to record sounds as indentations on a sheet of paper.

A year later, he turned his focus towards creating a solution that produced safe and inexpensive electric light. Keep in mind that at the time, this was a challenge that scientists had been grappling with for over 50 years.

Edison believed that he could find the answer, so with the help of financial backers, he set up the Edison Electric Light Company and started research and development.

Early on, Edison ran into a hiccup after hiccup in his attempts to produce the incandescent lightbulb. But two key breakthroughs in 1879 and 1880 helped him create the world's first affordable and long-lasting lightbulb in 1881.

It was reported that he had tried over 10,000 different combinations and techniques before a viable finished product was created. Describing his stream of failures, Edison famously said, "I haven't failed, I've just found 10,000 ways that don't work."

When we experience constant failure, it can be easy to get jaded and develop a negative mindset. It's easy to feel like the world is against us and that things are happening to us and not for us.

But the truth is that everything that happens in your life does happen for you. Whatever pain and failure you're struggling through right now is happening for a reason – it's trying to teach you valuable lessons that can be used for your breakthrough.

You may not see it that way, but it's the truth.

Story – 04

JK Rowling's Inspirational Story About Rejection

It's impossible to leave J.K. Rowling off of this list of true motivational stories given all that she experienced when trying to fulfil her dream of becoming a writer.

In 1994 J.K. Rowling was divorced, jobless, and a single mother who suffered severe bouts of depression regularly. Through everything she was going through, one thing remained – her love of writing.

Barely surviving on unemployment benefits, she used every spare second she could to write her manuscript.

Eventually, the day finally came when her manuscript was completed. However, she still needed to find a publisher who was willing to take a chance on her.

She took her manuscript to the first publisher, and they said no. She took it to the second publisher, who also said no.

Twelve times, J.K. Rowling walked into the office of a publisher. And twelve times, she was told that her work simply wasn't good enough.

At this point, she was almost ready to quit. Rejection after rejection had taken its toll on her and she began questioning her ability as a writer.

However, eventually, her manuscript got accepted. The book that these publishers rejected was Harry Potter, which has now sold 500 million copies worldwide and has been turned into a movie series that's grossed billions of dollars.

A story like this makes you think – how many great artists and novelists have we lost because of the word no?

How many people have given up without realizing each failure was bringing them one step closer to success?

Rowling's story highlights the importance of not letting failures define who you are. After the 5th, 8th, or 11th rejection, it would have been very easy for Rowling to throw in the towel.

But because of her courage and persistence, the world was able to enjoy her work, and she was able to live her dream.

I hope that you took something valuable away from these stories and that they gave you a raw and real perspective on success.

Most people tend to believe that as long as they work hard and do the right things, everything will go according to plan. But the thing about hard work is that although it's necessary to achieve success, it doesn't protect us from the slings and arrows of life.

Success is a pursuit that never goes according to plan. As you chase your dreams, realize that there will be times when you want to give up.

There will be times when you're wondering whether or not to persevere through constant rejection. There may be times when you don't know whether or not you'll be able to pay your bills.

In these moments, it's important to keep your perspective and realize that others in your position have faced the same circumstances, possibly worse.

J.K. Rowling continued to meet with publishers despite rejection after rejection. Walt Disney still believed in his vision even after being forced to eat dog food to conserve money.

Even after failure #3,267, Thomas Edison continued to hold out hope that each failure was bringing him closer and closer to his ultimate goal.

So whatever you're trying to do with your life right now, all you have to do is stay on the path. Remember these true motivational stories about successful people.

Remember that behind every successful person, there are a lot of unsuccessful years.

Chapter – 07
Believe in Yourself

Believing in yourself means having confidence in your abilities. It means being able to trust yourself to do what you say you'll do and knowing that those efforts will result in the desired outcomes. That means that believing in yourself comes from a mixture of several key psychological experiences — experiences like **self-worth, self-confidence, self-trust, self-respect, autonomy,** and **environmental mastery**.

When we believe in ourselves, it can help us achieve our <u>goals</u>, <u>manifest our dreams</u>, and increase our well-being. But the flip side is also true. A lack of belief in ourselves means we are less likely to act, change, or push to make things better. When we expect we will fail, we are more likely to fail.

That means that believing in ourselves is kind of like the key that turns the ignition and starts the car. We can't go anywhere without it. Try as we might push ourselves forward, we're blocked because our thoughts, attitudes, and actions aren't in alignment with our goals. So, we either don't do what we need to do or we sabotage ourselves along the way, sometimes in obvious ways and sometimes in <u>unconscious</u> ways.

Do you know what the most dangerous lie in the world is?

Two simple words: **"I can't."**

It's the falsehood most people say over and over to persuade themselves not to take risks that might make them uncomfortable or cause them to experience some sort of perceived **"failure."**

But the thing about failure is, it's simply a lesson that's giving you the information you need to do a better job next time. And being uncomfortable simply means you're having a new experience that's requiring you to grow!

That's why it's so important to let go of the words **"I can't"** and **instead embrace the truth: you can achieve absolutely anything you can imagine** – IF you believe in yourself.

By cultivating self-belief and developing a positive thinking mindset, you'll gain the confidence you need to successfully navigate any situation that life throws your way.

When you believe in yourself, your self-confidence becomes a self-fulfilling prophecy. You will be that person who can show up and get results – and you absolutely will experience better outcomes in everything you do!

So I'd love to share some thoughts on how to believe in yourself and gain confidence in your ability to take risks, overcome challenges, and achieve ambitious goals that require you to stretch and master new skills.

It's time to eliminate self-doubt and discover your abilities to change your own life and create the reality you want!

How to Believe in Yourself?

As I mentioned above, believing in yourself includes things like self-worth, self-confidence, self-trust, autonomy, and environmental mastery. These concepts are related but different. So I think it's useful to learn about each of them. That way, we can explore which parts we struggle with and take more efficient action to start believing in ourselves more. That way we'll get more than the advice of "**just believe in yourself**" — you'll have the information to understand why you don't and the tools to start shifting this belief.

Here's a quick overview. We'll go into more depth below.

- ➢ **Self-worth** is the sense that you have value as a human being.
- ➢ **Self-confidence** is a positive attitude about your abilities, qualities, and judgment.
- ➢ **Self-trust** is faith that you can rely on yourself.
- ➢ **Autonomy** is feeling able to choose and direct your behaviour.
- ➢ **Environmental mastery** is your belief that your efforts can result in the changes you desire.

These are some of the key components involved in believing in yourself. Maybe you struggle with just one of them or maybe you struggle with all of them. But by understanding where your struggles lie, it'll be easier to start shifting your attitudes about yourself.

Which Components of Self-Belief Do You Struggle with?

To better understand where you're getting stuck with self-belief, ask yourself these questions:

Self-worth: Do you value yourself as a human being? Do you agree that you're no worse than any other person?

Self-confidence: Do you feel good about your skills and abilities? Do you feel good about your personal qualities? Do you feel good about your judgment and decision-making?

Self-trust: Can you rely on yourself? Can you trust that you'll do what you say you'll do?

Autonomy: Do you feel free to do what you want to do? Do you believe that no one can stop you from reaching your dreams?

Environmental mastery: When you take action, do you believe that it will lead to the results you desire? Do you believe that you're effective in getting the things you want?

If you answered "**no**" or were leaning towards "**no**" to any of these questions, those are likely the areas that thwart your ability to believe in yourself.

For example, I struggle most with environmental mastery and autonomy. It's because I've had so many experiences where I was ineffective in getting what I wanted despite my best efforts. These experiences taught me to doubt myself.

What about you? What do you struggle with? Can you identify things that happened in your past that taught you to doubt yourself in the ways listed above?

Question Your Self-Doubts to Cultivate Self-Belief

Once you've identified your unsupportive self-beliefs, question these beliefs by talking back to your inner voice. If you feel like you have no value, tell yourself, "You are a valuable, amazing, person who deserves to live a good life." Or, if you don't feel confident, remind yourself of your good qualities and skills.

Positive self-talk like this has been shown to improve our performance. By saying positive things to ourselves, we can start to rewrite our internal scripts. We can slowly but surely start to develop new scripts in our minds that are a bit more like cheerleaders and a bit less like jerks. And this helps us shift our beliefs.

5 More Tips to Believe in Yourself

above, we have covered some of the main keys to believing in yourself. Here are some more tips and strategies to boost self-esteem and well-being to help you believe in yourself more.

- ➢ Develop a more **mindset**.
- ➢ Learn **how to manifest** what you want.
- ➢ Try a **self-compassion exercise**.
- ➢ Imagine being your **best self**.
- ➢ Map out your **long-term goals**.

THE IMPACT OF BELIEVING IN YOURSELF

Believing in yourself affects everything you do. Everything. From your professional life to your personal life to your solitary life. In your relationship with yourself and your relationships with others. In the choices you make and in the dreams you dream. How you view yourself, how you measure your value, how you assess your potential and how you determine your worth all combine to create the life you will live

Benefits of Believing in Yourself

Let's dig into the psychological benefits of cultivating self-belief – and developing a positive mindset that allows you to have faith in your ability to attain a much higher level of personal and professional success.

Self-Confidence is Key

If you don't believe in yourself, no one else will. That may sound harsh but it's true.

When you're full of self-doubt and overly critical of your behaviour, people will tend to assume that you know what you're talking about.

Either they think there is probably a good reason for you to have low self-esteem, or they'll read your negative self-talk and lack of self-trust as proof you haven't yet developed the growth mindset required to get you to where you want to be in life. And because they know you have more work to do, they'll be less likely to give you the support to move rapidly forward.

The fact is, you are the only one who can build self-confidence and cultivate the positive attitude you need to believe in yourself and succeed in life. And the good thing is, it can be easier than you think.

Small shifts in your mindset can help you develop self-love and self-trust and gain the high self-esteem you need to attract people to your vision and become unstoppable!

START BELIEVING IN YOURSELF BY BELIEVING IN YOURSELF

Too often we look at others and compare our worth to theirs. Or we look at our past and use it to determine our future. Neither of these has any bearing on what your life can be. No matter how successful and talented you deem everyone else to be or how many times you think you have failed when you believe that the future is whatever you choose to make it, that is exactly what it begins to be.

You will decide what jobs to apply for based on your belief in your ability to secure them and do them well. You will pursue promotions based on your belief that you have earned them and that you are ready for the next level. You will take chances, risks and opportunities based on your belief that they are valuable for your growth and that you are valuable and deserving of them. You will negotiate and ask for raises based on your confidence in doing so and your belief that the money is rightfully yours. You will learn to confront people and situations because being liked by others is far less important to you than being respected and liked by yourself and believing in your strength to do the right thing. You will lead with confidence and vision because you recognize how great you can be, even if your skills are not yet where you would like them to be.

BELIEVING IN YOURSELF STARTS BEGINS AND ENDS WITH YOUR MINDSET

And like everything else, it all starts with your mindset, with the conversations you have with yourself and the messages you choose to believe. You can tell yourself that you are simply not good at something or you can tell yourself that you can get better at anything you dedicate your energy to. You can talk yourself out of applying for a job you want because you think you will never get it, or you can prepare a powerful cover letter explaining why you are a fabulous fit for the position. You can tell yourself that you are just not good at public speaking or confrontation or Microsoft Excel or you can invest in your growth to get better at what will help you shine.

So how do you believe in yourself in moments or even a lifetime when you don't? Some people will tell you to fake it until you do not have to take it anymore. If that work for you? But more than faking it, I think being honest and starting exactly where you are is more effective. When I quit smoking, the most powerful advice I ever received was that all I had to do to quit smoking was to not smoke. Believing in yourself works the same way. If you want to start doing it, you simply need to start doing it. It is a process and it may be slower and harder than you would prefer., but know that you will get better at it if you choose.

One Step Closer to Success

When you believe in yourself, it's much easier to take the first big step that will bring you closer to your goal. And then the next step. And the next!

Self-doubt will try to convince you that your next step will cause you to stumble and fall. But, if you feel confident and have a high sense of self-worth, you're more likely to trust your inner compass and have faith that you will lead yourself in the direction of your goals.

Low self-esteem sees only danger in its future while high self-esteem envisions endless possibilities.

Encourages You to Keep Trying

Even when you do run into challenges and setbacks when you have a high level of self-belief you're able to rebound faster and figure out a way to resolve the situation successfully so you can get back on track toward all the amazing things you want to accomplish in your life.

You will also find it easier to enlist people to your cause and get the support you need to overcome any obstacle – because the people who can help you will see how deeply you believe in yourself and trust that their efforts to assist you won't be wasted.

Factors Preventing You from Trusting Yourself

The first step to overcoming low self-confidence and negative thinking is to recognize the factors that are holding you back from developing the self-trust and positive thinking you need to believe in yourself.

Here are some of the reasons people struggle to cultivate the positive attitude and self-confidence required to reach their desired finish line.

Comparing Yourself

Comparison inevitably leads to unhappiness. We will always notice something the other person has that we don't have and feel like our life is somehow "lesser than" as a result of not possessing that thing.

But the truth is, when you compare yourself to others, you don't see their whole truth!

They may be struggling in ways you can't see or imagine. And even if they are thriving, that doesn't mean that you can't.

Happiness isn't a zero-sum game. The happier and more successful you are, the happier and more successful all of us are.

Past Experiences

Oftentimes, the reason you find it hard to believe in yourself or appreciate your positive qualities is due to experiences you had in your childhood that damaged your self-trust.

Someone you trusted told you, "You don't have what it takes to do that!" and made you question your self-worth. Because when people you trust say "you can't," you tend to believe them.

If events in your past have caused you to limit your self-belief and think negative thoughts about your self-worth, a great way to counteract those unsupportive thoughts is to engage in a regular mindset practice.

Current Relationships

Perhaps you're in a relationship with someone whose influence makes it hard for you to believe in yourself. I'm talking about the kind of person who makes you believe you don't have what it takes to change your life for the better. Hang around with someone like that for long enough and you're bound to start believing them!

So if you struggle to believe in yourself, take a close look at the people you spend time with. Do they support you and cheer you on as you work toward creating the good life you dream of? When you express self-doubt, do they reassure you that you're awesome and can achieve anything you set your mind to? Or do they encourage your low-self confidence in obvious ways, such as constantly pointing out what they see as your weaknesses or past mistakes?

If you feel like they're trying to hold you back and make you feel bad about yourself, it's time to start compassionately exploring how to limit your time with them.

Self-Sabotage

Regardless of how other people in our lives treat us, you are always your own biggest enemy! This may sound odd but it's true: you can't control the words, thoughts, and actions of other people but you **CAN** control your own.

You're the only one who can. And when you insist on sabotaging your efforts by procrastinating, dwelling in self-doubt, and ignoring opportunities to take action that will help you cultivate confidence and believe in yourself, you're choosing (consciously or unconsciously) to keep yourself small.

You may think what you're doing is protecting yourself from the risk of failure, but all you're doing is preventing yourself from discovering what you're capable of accomplishing.

Change your self-talk

Once you've identified your unsupportive self-beliefs, question these beliefs by talking back to **your <u>inner voice</u>.** If you feel like you have no value, tell yourself, "You are a valuable, amazing, person who deserves to live a good life." Or, if you don't feel confident, remind yourself of your positive qualities and skills. Positive self-talk like this has been shown to improve our performance. By saying positive things to ourselves, we can start to rewrite our internal scripts.

Steps to Believe in Yourself

Now that you're aware of the roadblocks that have been making it hard for you to believe in yourself more, it's time to take action. Overcome those challenges and start exercising your power to build confidence in your ability to accomplish your big goals and create a life you love.

You always have the choice to start shifting your thoughts in a new direction and rewrite your internal scripts to cultivate belief in your ability to do whatever you want in life.

Here are steps that can help you make it happen:

Trust it's Possible

Engage in regular positive self-reflection where you list absolutely everything you have accomplished in your life.

Prove to yourself that you are capable of setting and achieving goals and taking risks and successfully surviving them.

You may even want to start a positive self-talk practice to cultivate faith in your abilities and get used to seeing yourself as someone who dreams big and has the power to bring your bold vision to life.

Build self-trust

We often think of trust as something we have for others. But we can also have trust in ourselves. Having (or not having) this trust in ourselves has similar implications as having (or not having) trust in others. For example, when we trust someone, we're honest with them, we can count on them, and we are confident in them doing what's best for us.

So what might it mean when we don't trust ourselves? Well, maybe we don't want to be honest with ourselves because we're not sure what we'll do with that information. Maybe we can't count on ourselves to do the things we tell ourselves we'll do. Or, maybe we're afraid that we'll do things to harm ourselves instead of helping ourselves.

It may sound odd when spelt out like this, but many of us do indeed have self-trust issues. For example, maybe we've told ourselves a thousand times that we are going to start exercising... but we never do it. So how likely is it that we'd trust ourselves to start a new exercise program? Not very likely.

Visualize It: See What You Want, Get What You See

Regular visualization allows you to see the kind of future you're working towards. Not only does this help you make sure you're always moving forward in the right direction, but it also helps you keep your goals top of mind even when a million other distractions are vying for your energy and attention.

One way to stay focused on your vision is by creating your motivational vision board. A vision board is a graphic representation of exactly what you want in life.

It can include pictures from magazines or ones you've downloaded online, as well as motivational words and sayings to remind you of your values, purpose, and desired experience.

Put it somewhere you can see it every day to give yourself a powerful visual reminder of the future you're working towards.

Act "As If": Where Do You See Yourself in 5 Years?

One of the most effective ways to develop a positive success mindset is to act as if you're already the kind of person who has created the life you dream of living.

Ask yourself: If you had already achieved your dream, what kind of person would you be? Whom would you have as friends? What type of clothes would you be wearing? How would you act? How would you treat others? Would you tithe a portion of your income to your church or favourite charities?

Whatever actions you identify, start taking them now.

By acting "as if," you'll become capable of creating the success you want – and this will trigger your subconscious mind to find creative ways to achieve your goals.

You will start noticing anything that will help you succeed. Best of all, you'll start acting on these opportunities, because you will have the confidence that your efforts will yield great results.

Take Action Toward Your Goals

I've noticed this is where a lot of people get stuck. You can understand all these principles, and you can set your goals, say your affirmations, and do your visualizations, but ultimately nothing happens if you don't act on them.

The biggest reason most people don't achieve their goals and realize their dream is that they don't take action, and the number one reason people don't take action is fear. But fear is normal!

Courage isn't the absence of fear – it's the willingness to keep moving forward into the unknown despite your fear. You're able to experience the fear and take action anyway.

So how do you do that? You start small and take tiny achievable steps in the right direction.

Allow yourself to be curious and cut yourself some slack if you stumble and fall. Just get back up, learn from the lesson, and keep going, trusting that you will gain the skills you need to reach your destination as you proceed on your journey.

Believe in Yourself by Learning to Master Your World

Environmental mastery is all about taking effective action to achieve the results you want. If we've failed in the past or struggled to achieve the goals we've set for ourselves despite doing our best, we might not believe in our ability to do what we set our minds to. We might not believe we can do it because in the past we didn't do it. And that's understandable.

If we struggle here, we might have a nagging feeling that our best isn't good enough. Why belief in ourselves—why try— when it doesn't seem to work?

In the research, this type of phenomenon is sometimes referred to as learned helplessness. Early research showed that when animals were repeatedly exposed to electric shocks, they stopped trying to get away after a while, even though it was now possible to get away (Maier & Seligman, 1976). They had learned from repeated failures that no matter what they did, they could not change their situation. They could not master their environment. As a result, they no longer believed in themselves.

A few older studies explored ways to reverse learned helplessness but provided few clear answers. Overall, it seems that setting small, achievable goals can help people regain a sense of environmental mastery. For example, one study showed elderly folks how to grow and take care of a plant to boost environmental mastery. Just the act of taking control of your environment in some small way can help.

In general, we need to make good use of effective **goal-setting** strategies and be sure not to set overly ambitious goals. Setting goals that are out of reach may just reinforce the belief that we cannot meet our goals or achieve the results we desire.

This is what I struggle with, so I know that these are tough beliefs to overcome. But I have found some early success with breaking my goals down into small chunks that I know I can achieve. My goal for today is to finish this article... and I know I can do that. Repeatedly having these small successes helps me regain my belief in myself.

Believing in ourselves involves a bit more than just forcing ourselves to develop self-love and start pursuing our goals. It's more a matter of seeing where we're stuck and compassionately exploring how to get unstuck.

BELIEVING IN YOURSELF DOESN'T MEAN IGNORING CHALLENGES

To my naysayers and those who are used to focusing on what they believe to be wrong and in need of fixing, rest assured that believing in yourself does not in any way necessitate a delusion of self or a pretension of perfection. We all have our struggles and challenges. The reason I am pointing for this focus and dedication solely on strengths and self-belief is that too many of us already spend far too much time focusing on that which we feel we lack. Too often, those around us, both personally and professionally focus on these things too. I am not the least bit concerned that you are not spending enough time on these areas. My heart breaks when I think about how much you probably do.

So start doing something different. Start believing in yourself. Right this minute. I promise, if you keep at it and learn to fully embrace your potential, you will begin to live a life you enjoy and are proud of. I believe in you. Now go start believing in yourself!

Believing in ourselves involves a bit more than just forcing ourselves to develop self-love and start pursuing our goals. It's more a matter of seeing where we're stuck and compassionately exploring how to get unstuck. Hopefully, these were some useful tips to get started.

Do you know the story of the elephant in the circus?

While still a baby, the elephant was tied by its leg to a stake driven into the ground. Naturally, they didn't like it and tried to escape for a long time but the rope and the stake were too strong for him. So the elephant tired from the failure gave up.

Later, when it grew up, the elephant remembered all the efforts and the failures and still believed it could not escape from the rope, standing in the same place despite the fact it could then easily escape as it has extraordinary strength.

It sounds unbelievable this gigantic and powerful animal limited its capacity by failure in the past. But it happens also to us, human beings.

We certainly all have some tasks that we tried and failed in the past. But we are smarter than elephants and we know that we grow over time and become smarter and stronger. We know we cannot allow our failures to become limiting beliefs. Unlike the elephant story, we learn from our mistakes and failures, we are smart enough to lose the fear of failing again and believe that we are now more capable.

So, overcome your fear, break your limits and realize that you are capable of accomplishing anything you want.

It's time to face your challenges, don't you think so?

Don't give in to the limitations of society. Believe that you can achieve everything you want to!

If you are reading this, I will tell you that it's very difficult to move forward holding the mountain on your shoulders, it's time to release the weight which is dragging you back. Say this to yourself I am learning every day to allow the space between where I am and where I want to be and inspire me and not terrify me.

Make a practice of asking for what you want. No self-imposed guilt. No Self-imposed shame. Do not be afraid to voice what you desire or what you deserve. Be, Live, Enjoy.

Chapter – 08
Finding beauty through the pain

(Turn your problems into opportunities)

When faced with problems or setbacks in your life, what is your immediate reaction? If you're like most people, your first impulse is to complain. "Why did this have to happen to me? What am I going to do now? My plans are ruined! How to turn your problems into opportunities to change your life, so that you realize that, looking at them from another point of view, they can be beautiful lucky strokes for you.

Surely you have had bad times in which life has hit you hard. In those moments, your world is flooded with worries. When you think that nothing worse can happen, a catastrophe happens.

And when you feel that all that suffering tightens you more and more inside you, the last thing you think about is turning your problems into opportunities.

When situations seem to be difficult and shattered, we can still keep a **positive attitude** and see those problems as **opportunities**. If we see it from a larger perspective, it is all a learning path, and on this path, we make many mistakes and face many problems. But we should never give up, and we should be **optimistic**.

Everyone finds it discouraging when their present conditions do not match their planned and desirable expectations. Problems occur repeatedly, and even the most motivated people get discouraged.

However, after the initial disappointment wears off, you have a choice to make. You can either wallow in misery and dwell on the negative aspects of your situation or you can find the benefit or lesson that the problem is offering. Yes, you'll probably face a period of uncertainty or struggle, but there's always a flip side to the difficulty. You see, a "problem" is often not a problem at all. It may actually be an opportunity. For instance, a problem may point out an adjustment you can make to improve certain conditions in your life. Without the problem, you never would have **ATTITUDE IS EVERYTHING** taken this positive action.

For example, you probably know or have heard about someone who lost his or her job and then went on to start a successful business. Often, that person will tell you that if he or she hadn't been laid off, the new business would never have been started. What started as an adversity and ended up as a golden opportunity? How about the times you were convinced that a particular job was perfect for you; you had a great interview and just couldn't wait for the offer? But the offer never came — someone else got the job. You were devastated! Days or months later a new job came along, and you realized that the first position was much less desirable than the one that came along later. The earlier rejection was, in fact, a blessing. Another example is the deal on the "dream house" which falls through... only to be replaced by something even better.

Understand the situation

The skill of turning a problem into an opportunity is an art that is practised by a clear and open mindset.

We should accept the situation and search for things that we can change and turn into a source of new opportunities.

We cannot control everything happening around us, and there is no need to feel bad when unexpected problems come in our way.

Focus on the solution, not on the problem

We should focus on the possible results of the situation more than on the problem. The problem will not give us anything but the path of finding the solution can open many new opportunities for us.

Concentrate on the solution, not the problem

Concentrate on the possible outcomes of the specific situation, not on the problem by itself. The problem has nothing to give you, but the way of finding a solution for it can open many doors of possibilities in front of you.

Problems put us in places which we would never get into if not for the unexpected outcomes. This challenge is the best way to see ourselves completely out of our comfort zone and to test our ability to take the unexpected and turn it into something desirable, something of great value for us.

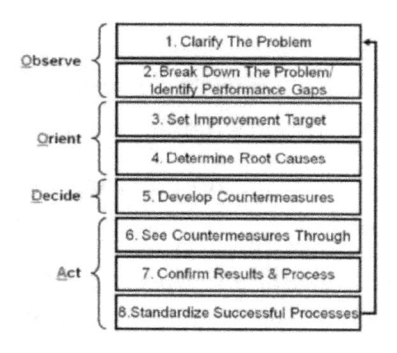

Observe	1. Clarify The Problem
	2. Break Down The Problem/ Identify Performance Gaps
Orient	3. Set Improvement Target
	4. Determine Root Causes
Decide	5. Develop Countermeasures
Act	6. See Countermeasures Through
	7. Confirm Results & Process
	8. Standardize Successful Processes

Look at your problems from a different point of view

If you want to turn your problems into an opportunity to grow, the starting point is to recognize the situation you are in.

Don't try to run away from it, or push it aside trying to get it to go away, because that just won't happen.

You must accept it, but without seeing that situation as a problem, but as a push to go ahead and learn from it.

Realize that as people, when we think of something as a problem, we are telling our mind that it is something that has no solution.

Thoughts like" I can't, "This can't be fixed, "I won't be able to get out of this" begin to cross our heads, and in this way, we will only be able to block ourselves and prevent ourselves from finding a remedy for that.

However, seeing it from another point of view, you will be able to prove to yourself that this situation does have a solution because you will be able to see it from a much more objective perspective.

Think of it as a challenge instead of a problem. The moment you do this; you will notice that your mental attitude changes completely.

When you look at it as a challenge, your brain, unconsciously and automatically, will tell you, "Maybe I can do it, yes I can overcome it."

There, without you hardly realizing it, you will be raising your motivation, seeing a possible solution that can become something real.

The wheel of your imagination will start looking for alternatives, and you will draw from within the strength you need to solve it and face that challenge.

Judge the available options

Observe what we can do. Create **a list** of all options that we have and create an action plan then act according to it. Whatever the situation is, we should always continue to move on and continue our journey.

Take responsibility and do not play a blame game

Blame and finger-pointing only cause anger and make the problem bigger. We should **take responsibility** and take the challenge to solve it. Self-blaming is good. It is good to take ownership than to blame others.

Example of turning a problem into the opportunity

This is one is on the famous people who overcame incredible obstacles Steve Jobs' life is the **best real-life example** from which we can learn, developing such a mindset of turning problems into opportunities.

We all know Steve Jobs as the marketing genius and co-founder of Apple, one of the most successful companies in the world today.

Contrary to many people on this list, Jobs was a fairly quick succession. By the age of 25, his net worth was over $100 million.

What you probably don't know is that he was fired from Apple, the company he co-founded, by a man named John Sculley. Ironically, just a few years earlier Jobs had hired Scully to help run the company.

Jobs wanted the CEO title, but the board felt like he was too young and too difficult to work with, so they ousted him.

How would you feel if you were fired right in your prime from the very company that you built from the ground up? Jobs was humiliated, but he didn't see this situation as permanent – **just a temporary setback.**

Almost immediately after getting fired from Apple, he founded a company called NeXT. He poured all of his efforts into building an operating system that would change the world, and he succeeded.

Realizing the value of what Jobs was doing at NeXT, Apple ended up buying them for $429 million. A few months later, Jobs was named interim CEO and then eventually acquired the coveted CEO title that he had gotten fired for aiming at 12 years prior.

After the biggest failure of his career, all it took was twelve years of struggle and work to reach his ultimate goal.

Visualize yourself overcoming that problem

This is the critical point to turn your problems into opportunities: focus on the great satisfaction you will feel once you have overcome your challenges.

Every time there is an obstacle in your life, and you try to run away from it because you don't know or don't want to face it, how do you feel afterwards?

Surely you are disappointed with yourself, and your spirit will drop because you have not been able to face it, and you regret not having done something at the time to find a solution.

But if instead you look at the problem from another perspective, and see it as an opportunity to change your life for the better, you will have enough strength to go for it and overcome it.

And when you have succeeded, you will feel an enormous sense of improvement that will make you proud of having been able to do it and not having given up despite those circumstances.

For this reason, no matter what happens in your life, it is essential that you focus on the result, and how it will make you feel once it has happened so that from the beginning, your mind starts working in a more optimistic state.

Only in this way can you take it for what it is: the best opportunity to grow as a person, and to improve yourself by becoming someone better.

So don't give up on your problems, and take action to beat them and take advantage of them. Remember that staying with your arms crossed will never achieve anything.

Finding beauty through the pain

Overcoming Obstacles:

Stephen Hawking Defies the ALS Odds

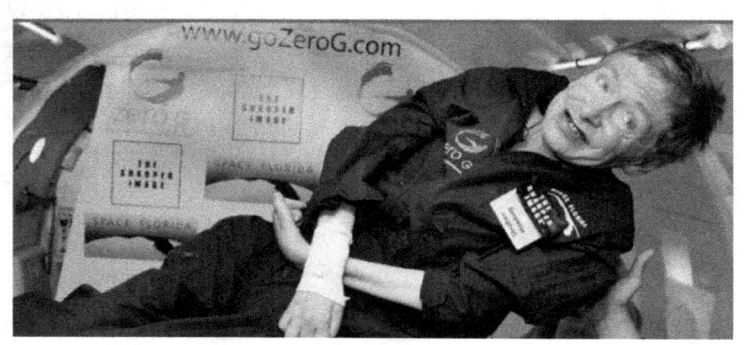

This is one is on a famous person who overcame incredible obstacles, <u>*failed many times*</u> *or defied grim odds in order to succeed.*

Long before the neurodegenerative disease <u>ALS (amyotrophic lateral sclerosis)</u> became more well-known thanks to the <u>Ice Bucket Challenge</u>, it was very much a part of physicist Stephen Hawking's life. In fact, it was a significant challenge that Hawking lived with for more than 50 years, which is astounding given the debilitating nature of the disease and the fact it is usually fatal within five years of a diagnosis.

Getting the ALS Diagnosis

Hawking was just 21 and studying <u>cosmology</u> at the University of Cambridge when his father noticed he was tripping and falling frequently, so he sent his son to a medical clinic where he took a series of tests. Eventually, the diagnosis came back—he had ALS, also known as <u>Lou Gehrig's</u> disease, and doctors estimated he had two and half years left to live.

A type of <u>motor neuron disease</u>, ALS causes nerve cells in the brain and spinal cord to weaken and eventually die. When these motor neurons die, the brain can no longer control muscle movement and the body is paralyzed. Symptoms start as muscle twitching and weakness in the arms and legs and slight slurring of speech. Eventually, ALS affects the muscles needed to move, speak, eat, and breathe.

Gaining a New Perspective

The news was, of course, devastating, but Hawking derived hope from the fact that he still had some time left and he began to take a new interest in his studies and his research. "I was bored with life before my illness," he said. "There had not seemed to be anything worth doing." His illness, as is the case with many major life obstacles, seems to have spurred him on to achievements he may not have reached otherwise as he now showed a new intensity for his work. Thinking he would die soon gave Hawking a new perspective on his life. "In fact," Hawking has said, "although there was a cloud hanging over my future, I found, to my surprise, that I was enjoying life in the present more than before."

Though extremely intelligent, Hawking ranked third from the bottom of his class in high school and tended to put only minimum time into his studies in college before his illness, despite graduating with honours from Oxford University at the age of 17.

Focusing on Abilities

After his diagnosis, Hawking began studying <u>black holes</u> and the origins of the universe. As his health diminished—he began using a wheelchair—his life and his research flourished. He married in 1965 and had three children, and his research received public recognition in 1974 when he demonstrated that black holes are not information vacuums as once thought, but they emit a stream of particles. His "Hawking Radiation" discovery provided essential information into how gravity relates to other forms of energy. His discovery and publications made him famous in the scientific community and eventually around the world. He was soon named a fellow of the Royal Society, earned the prominent Albert Einstein Award and received the Pius XI Gold Medal for Science from Pope Paul VI. His subsequent theories continue to further the world's understanding of the universe.

His disease continued to progress, however, and by the mid-1970s he needed more care and his speech was so slurred only his family could understand him. But still, he learned to manage and overcome the significant challenges of his condition. In 1985, Hawking had another health scare when he contracted pneumonia. He became so ill that his doctors put him into a drug-induced coma and asked his wife if she wanted to stop life support efforts. Instead, she had him flown back to Cambridge where he received a tracheotomy, which left him without the ability to speak at all. "The weeks of intensive care that followed were the darkest of my life," Stephen admits in a new film about his life.

He did make a full recovery, however, allowing him to finish writing A Brief History of Time, which sold 10 million copies around the world. Although he continues to defy the odds of living with ALS for so long, his condition is always challenging as he needs 24-hour care and can communicate only with the aid of a computer device, which he operates using the remaining muscles he still controls in his cheek. "For the last three years I have been on full-time ventilation," Hawking recently told 200 delegates at the European Global

Tracheostomy Collaborative in London, "but this has not prevented me from leading a full and active life."

Benefiting from a Positive Outlook

From the time he was diagnosed, Hawking did not let his condition stop him from achieving his goals. "I am quite often asked: 'How do you feel about having ALS?' The answer is, not a lot," Hawking said. "I try to lead as normal a life as possible, and not think about my condition, or regret the things it prevents me from doing, which are not that many." Although it would be easy to think about what this disease has cost him, Hawking chose to focus on all that he still has. His brilliant mind remained unaffected by ALS, so he could continue to enjoy the benefits of that. Hawking had 12 honorary degrees and he received multiple awards, medals and prizes. He has even appeared on several television shows, including *Star Trek: The Next Generation, The Simpsons,* and *The Big Bang Theory.* There have been documentaries about his life and a film called *The Theory of Everything.* He also co-authored a children's book with his daughter called <u>George's Secret Key to the Universe</u> to educate young children about the universe and black holes.

It is not known why Hawking defied the odds and lived with this deadly disease for so long, though the fact he contracted ALS at such a young age is thought to contribute to his ability to survive longer than those diagnosed over the age of 50. Generally, fewer than 10 per cent of ALS sufferers live longer than ten years, however. "I have been lucky that my condition has progressed more slowly than is often the case," Hawking said. **"But it shows that one need not lose hope."**

Hawking's life story serves as an inspiration to children and adults, especially those who are struggling with a chronic or serious illness. His lessons of positive thinking, focusing on what can be accomplished, taking advantage of the time provided, and ignoring the difficulties, can be taught in all areas of life.

GROW LIKE A LOTUS

As a lotus flower is born in water, grows in water and rises out of the water to stand above it unsoiled, so I, born in the world, raised in the world having overcome the world, live unsoiled by the world. – Gautama Buddha

Just like the lotus, we too have the ability to rise from the mud, bloom out of darkness, and radiate into the world." – Unknown

The lotus has been called the beautiful survivor. Maybe you can relate to that. The lotus pushes its way through the mud, rising toward the sun's light. As the lotus bud first emerges at the surface of the water and basks in the sunlight, the first petal opens.

A lotus is a survivor, it rises from the dark muddy waters and finds the warmth and nourishment of the Light. As the bud hits the surface of the water and drinks in the sunlight, that single petal opens, signifying an achievement. Oftentimes in our busy lives, we overlook the smallest achievements. Each petal that opens is an achievement of survival, life, and opportunity. A lotus has strength and beauty, it can overcome all of its environmental obstacles and show the world its beauty.

Famous Jewish Buddhist Goldie Hawn says this precious bloom is her favourite. She writes: "The lotus is the most beautiful flower; whose petals open one by one. But it will only grow in the mud. In order to grow and gain wisdom, first, you must have the mud — the obstacles of life and its suffering. The mud speaks of the common ground that humans share, no matter what our stations in life. Whether we have it all or we have nothing, we are all faced with the same obstacles: sadness, loss, illness, dying and death. If we are to strive as human beings to gain more wisdom, more kindness, and more compassion, we must have the intention to grow as a lotus and open each petal one by one."

According to one story, the muddier and more opaque the water the more resplendent the Lotus flower when it rises to life, to the water's surface–a gift for all who see. May the muck and struggle of our lives yield such beauty.

Chapter – 09
Purpose In Life

"The mystery of human existence lies not in just staying alive, but in finding something to live for." – Fyodor Dostoyevsky

Some mornings when we wake up, everything feels futile and we are haunted by the question **"What is the purpose of life?"**

Sometimes you feel that there's something deeper you could be a part of. You feel the pull towards something, but you can't exactly pin it down—it eludes you and frustrates you.

That's because you are not sure of your purpose in life.

The answer to "**What is my purpose**" is not simple or straight. It can be a sort of awakening or an epiphany.

Life is an opportunity to be happy and grow as a person. It's about finding where you fit in this world and what you want to do with your time here on Earth.

When we find our purpose, we can move forward with confidence because the struggle becomes worth it when you know that there's something bigger in your life than just existing.

You might have heard stories from writers or musicians who have felt their calling their entire lives; the Mozarts of the world who have pursued their passions from the moment they were out of the womb. Deep down, you wish you had this "knowing" to pull you forward.

Frankly, you do: all it takes is a little digging to uncover the truth when you start asking how to find your purpose. In today's fast-paced, technology-filled world where we are being pulled in many directions at once, finding the purpose of life seems more important than ever.

Many people spend their lives reacting to situations instead of being proactive and figuring out the needs and values that drive them. Even when they think they know their purpose, they often mistake it for a short-term goal. Many others who are asking themselves this question truly want to find meaning – but they have no idea how to find purpose in life.

Purpose can guide life decisions, influence behaviour, shape goals, offer a sense of direction, and create meaning. For some people, the purpose is connected to vocation—meaningful, satisfying work. For others, their purpose lies in their responsibilities to their family or friends. Others seek meaning through spirituality or religious beliefs. Some people may find their purpose clearly expressed in all these aspects of life.

The purpose will be unique for everyone; what you identify as your path may be different from others. What's more, your purpose can shift and change throughout life in response to the evolving priorities and fluctuations of your own experiences.

WHY YOU'RE SEEKING THE PURPOSE OF LIFE

Tony Robbins says, **"If you're not growing, you're dying"** – which is why growth is addictive to many of us. We naturally only feel fulfilled when we're improving ourselves or our lives in some way. Everything in life is calling us to grow. When we stop growing, we start feeling pain, fear and anxiety. We are then susceptible to envy as we look around and see what everyone else has that we don't. Instead of asking "What is my purpose in life?" we start coveting status, material goods and power. But all those things will ultimately leave you feeling empty.

Goals, like buying a house or opening a business, yield a sense of achievement and are essential to living the life you desire. Purpose takes those goals to an even higher level. In Date with Destiny, Tony Robbins tells everyone in the room: "I will tell you right now, there's one word that will give you happiness, one. You'll remember it as long as you live: progress. Progress equals happiness. Achieving goals does not equal happiness." So if you're asking yourself, "What is my purpose?" what you're asking for is progress – a true sense of fulfilment. And fulfilment isn't a luxury or leisure activity – it's a necessity.

What is the Purpose of Life?

Finding your purpose in life adds psychological and emotional improvements and satisfaction to your life. You want more zest, more flavour, more fullness. In the strictest sense, you want to become a better person.

You want to wake up excited, jumping out of bed with a thirst for life that you haven't felt since you were a child.

Think of uncovering your passion like the work of a master sculptor, slowly chipping away the stone to reveal the masterpiece underneath. Your life's purpose is this masterpiece, simply lurking beneath the surface, waiting to be released.

Successful people know that the fastest way to learn how to find your purpose is through the art of introspection: diving into the deeper essence of who you are to pull out the pieces to assemble the purpose puzzle.

Think of your life's purpose as a golden thread; for some, that thread comes in the form of a certain career or profession, while for others, it looks like a way of being or expression

Your purpose can be the driving force behind this. If you feel lost, your sense of purpose can be your connection to something larger, something that will allow you to truly make a difference.

Still, your purpose meaning, and "why" you need to find it might be different. Before we even leave the solid ground, you need this as your anchor, just in case things get foggy. To find it, answer this question:

Why do you want to find your purpose in life?

Write down or remember whatever comes up. It might be some of the above reasons, or it might be something entirely different. Whatever it is, hold it close and look at it.

BENEFITS OF KNOWING YOUR PURPOSE

Research shows that finding your purpose is linked to living longer. Researchers surveyed nearly 7,000 older adults on the relationship between mortality and finding your purpose. Participants who did not have a strong sense of meaning in their lives were more than twice as likely to die prematurely as those who had figured out their purpose in life. Having a sense of purpose also reduced the incidence of cardiovascular events like heart attack and stroke.

These results were universal, even when controlled for income, race, gender and education level. Researchers concluded that finding your purpose helps you live longer. It's also essential for happiness and fulfilment.

Achieving goals may not help you find your purpose in life, but knowing your purpose can help you achieve your goals. When you truly know your purpose, you'll experience a sense of clarity like never before as you're able to connect what you want to achieve to your ultimate fulfilment. You'll feel passionate, driven and laser-focused. You'll stop battling with the past and the future and start living in the present – and that's the greatest gift you can give yourself.

have you ever woken up in a dark room with no source of light at all? Did you manage to do anything worthwhile? That's how living a life without a clear purpose is.

The majority of people live their lives in this manner. You need to find your purpose to have a meaningful life.

Here is the importance of finding your purpose and how it can help you improve the quality of your life:

HOW TO FIND PURPOSE IN LIFE?

There are many benefits of knowing your purpose – but how can you figure it out? It is a combination of the science of achievement and the art of fulfilment that creates the road to happiness and a life of meaning. To succeed in finding your purpose, you must master this balance.

SEARCH INWARD

The questions "What is my purpose in life?" and "How can I be happy?" are the same – and they have the same answer. You can never truly understand how to find your purpose by listening to others' opinions and seeking outside approval.

Everything you need is within yourself. The only thing holding you back is your own limiting beliefs. With each limiting belief you identify and replace with an empowering belief, you develop greater self-awareness. And when you're in control of your emotions, you're in control of your life.

PUT PURPOSE BEFORE GOALS

If you focus only on achieving short-term goals, you will never find your true passion or learn how to find your purpose. The goals you work toward must always be based on finding your purpose. If they're not, you'll only feel a fleeting sense of accomplishment and will soon be seeking something more. You won't be able to see that life is happening for you instead of to you.

When you set a goal, ask yourself: How will this help me feel more fulfilled? How does this relate to my purpose? Use a journal or a system like Tony's Rapid Planning Method to ensure you always keep your purpose top of mind.

FOCUS ON WHAT YOU HAVE

Developing a mindset is like opening your eyes to life: You will see beauty and goodness all around you. With this new perspective, your purpose in life becomes much clearer. You question less and less about how to find your purpose because you feel like you have more of the answers and that you are on the path to achieving meaningful goals.

When we focus on what we have, fear disappears and abundance appears. You'll stop living in fear that you're wasting your life and begin to attract positivity and joy.

Finding your purpose becomes an exciting journey, rather than a stressful goal.

TAKE OWNERSHIP OF YOUR LIFE

True fulfilment comes from **designing your own life**. This is how you unlock the extraordinary. To find your purpose, you must decide what's truly right, and know it in your heart and soul. You must not let yourself be driven by fear or anxiety. A decision made from fear is always the wrong decision. It will not help you understand "What is my purpose?" but instead confuse the issue even more.

To truly take ownership, you must stop playing the victim. Realize that every circumstance in your life is a result of your own decisions, not anyone else's. When you take responsibility for finding your purpose instead of blaming others, fulfilment follows.

THINK ABOUT WHAT BRINGS YOU JOY

Look back on your life and identify the times when you felt the most joy. Was it when you were connecting with your partner? Making a successful presentation at work? Creating art or helping others? When you discover what brings you joy, you usually discover where your passions lie.

Your abilities are connected to that sense of joy, so examine them, too: Can you pick up a pencil and sketch a lifelike portrait? Do your friends tell you that you're a great listener? When you look closely at the activities or skills that come naturally and also bring you joy, you'll likely stumble upon passions that you can turn into a profitable career.

Discover What You Are Most Passionate About

Everybody is passionate about something in life.

Finding your passion will help you answer what is the purpose of life. This isn't hard to do at all. You have to notice the things that you always look forward to.

You may or may not have a passion in life already. Regardless, there is always something that you wish you could spend more time doing.

Think about what things you want to be more eager about. Your life's purpose is hidden somewhere in these things.

If you focus on these actions daily, you will be living your life with purpose. It is at this point that feelings of happiness fill your life.

The more you do for others, the happier you will be.

Define Your True Priorities and Eliminate False Objectives

To live an extraordinary life, you need to live your life. Most people across the world live their lives according to the expectations of others. They build their habits and schedules around what their friends, families, and society want.

It takes confidence to live your life according to your priorities. This is especially true if your priorities are different from your loved ones. You need to figure out what matters most and the false objectives you are currently working towards.

Figure Out What Drains You

You need to think about the things that exhaust you mentally or physically. They don't have to be activities or tasks that you dislike. Once you can point out these tasks, it's time to stop doing them.

Indulging in purposeless activities drains your body and mind. You should consider delegating or eliminating them from your to-do list. Tiredness is a clear sign from your mind, body, and heart that the activity is not good for you.

It's important to run YOUR race, live YOUR life, focus on what matters to YOU, and build your life around YOUR vision.

Develop a Crystal-Clear Vision of the Life You Desire

As you define your true priorities, you can start developing a vision for the life you desire

What you believe about yourself–and what you believe is possible for yourself–affects how you show up every day to achieve your biggest goal.

Get clear about the life you desire and work on believing it's possible to achieve it.

TAKE TIME FOR YOURSELF

When you spend all your time running from one commitment to another, you never have time to just sit quietly and reconnect with yourself. Make sure you schedule enough personal time to reduce the noise and demands of the outer world and focus on what you want.

When you feel depleted searching for meaning in life, take a deep breath and centre yourself. Take time for self-care, whether that's a spa day or reading a book in the park or playing the guitar or whatever. It's by looking within that you're able to identify your values – the beliefs you hold dearest as a guiding force in life. You won't understand how to find your purpose without first taking a step back and relaxing your mind and body.

EMBRACE ACCEPTANCE

Part of finding your purpose is accepting your limitations. Instead of getting frustrated with yourself, give yourself a break. Get to know yourself bit by bit, taking the role of observer. As you practice self-compassion while building self-awareness, you're able to find the meaning you're seeking.

Self-compassion means being patient with yourself. Feeling lost in life can be a very disorienting feeling. You may feel frustrated, but be gentle with yourself. Everyone who has ever asked themselves "What is my purpose?" began from a place of uncertainty. Their hesitancy was what prompted them to dig deep and find greater meaning.

FIND YOUR COMMUNITY

Finding your purpose in life is often about discovering where you fit in. When we meet our "people," we feel like we are at home: relaxed and at ease, able to truly be ourselves. Your community can often help you discover how to find your purpose, or to live your purpose once you've found it.

To find your community, follow your passions. Join a volunteer group. Take a class to develop a skill you enjoy. Seek out support online. Find others who enjoy the same music, books or plays. The saying "You are who your friends are" is true – and when you find the right community, it's a good thing.

BE FLEXIBLE

"You can't connect the dots looking forward; you can only connect them looking backwards. So you have to trust that the dots will somehow connect in your future. You have to trust in something — your gut, destiny, life, karma, whatever. This approach has never let me down, and it has made all the difference in my life." - Steve Jobs

One of the hardest parts of learning how to find your purpose is letting go of old identities and interests that no longer serve us. Yet it's something that must be done. Your purpose in life is also likely to grow and change as you grow and change. You must be willing to be flexible and to listen to your innermost wants and needs.

Finding your purpose is a lifelong journey. Being flexible lets you grow in integrity while being true to yourself. When you develop your core values and stop seeking external affirmation, you'll find that the question of "What is my purpose in life?" is much easier to answer.

Every life has a purpose. We need to let go of the past. Live in the present. Do not waste today worrying about what will happen tomorrow. Embrace your true spirit, embrace and listen to grace and you be transformed at the moment. Do not fixate on what you want but give thanks for what you have.

Chapter – 10
Goal Setting.

Goal setting is everywhere in our world. We set goals for our careers, our health, and our lives in general. It seems modern society is always encouraging us to think about the next milestone. However, what we don't think about enough is the science and strategy of how to accomplish your goals. That's what this guide is here to do.

Many people feel as if they're adrift in the world. They work hard, but they don't seem to get anywhere worthwhile.

A key reason that they feel this way is that they haven't spent enough time thinking about what they want from life, and haven't set themselves formal goals. After all, would you set out on a major journey with no real idea of your destination? Probably not!

Do you ever feel like you're sleepwalking through life with no real idea of what you want?

Perhaps you know exactly what you want to achieve, but have no idea how to get there.

That's where goal setting comes in. Goals are the first step towards planning for the future, and play a fundamental role in the development of skills in various facets of life, from work to relationships and everything in between. They are the target at which we aim our proverbial arrow.

Understanding the importance of goals and the techniques involved in setting achievable goals paves the way for success.

What Is Goal Setting?

Goal setting is the process by which we achieve these goals. The importance of the goal-setting process should not go unappreciated. "Every person's life depends on the process of choosing goals to pursue; if you remain passive you are not going to thrive as a human being."

Goal setting can look different depending on an individual's lifestyle, values and definition of success. Your goals are unique to you and don't need to look like anyone else's.

The classic goal-setting definition boils down to the process of identifying something you want to accomplish and establishing measurable objectives and timeframes to help you achieve it. Goal setting can help you in any area of your life, from achieving financial freedom to adopting a healthy diet. When you learn how to set goals in one area of your life, it becomes easier to set them in other areas.

Setting progressive goals that allow small wins helps you move on to larger achievements. These small goals lead to progress, which is the only thing you need to feel fulfilled and happy.

WHY IS GOAL SETTING IMPORTANT?

Goal setting is the fundamental key to success. Whether it's increasing your intelligence, learning a new skill or rekindling a relationship, setting goals lets us create our future. It also helps us grow and expand, pushing ourselves to transform in ways that we never imagined. To feel fulfilled, we need to know and feel like we're working to achieve something. Tony

Robbins says, "Progress equals happiness," and setting goals gets us there.

Effective goal setting lets you measure progress, <u>overcome procrastination</u> and visualize your dreams. If you don't know what you want to accomplish, you can't create a plan to get there. Setting goals is the vehicle that will drive you to your desired destination.

Goal setting also keeps you accountable. Whether you're learning how to set goals at work or in your personal life, telling others about your goals makes you more likely to establish the patterns that will accomplish them.

Here we'll cover how to set goals to ensure you achieve them. You'll learn what makes a compelling goal as well as the steps you need to take to see them through.

Top-level athletes, successful businesspeople and achievers in all fields all set goals. Setting goals gives you long-term vision and short-term motivation. It focuses on your acquisition of knowledge and helps you to organize your time and your resources so that you can make the most of your life.

By setting sharp, clearly defined goals, you can measure and take pride in the achievement of those goals, and you'll see forward progress in what might previously have seemed a long pointless grind. You will also raise your self-confidence, as you recognize your ability and competence in achieving the goals that you've set.

Why Should We Set Goals in Life?

Lots of us have dreams. We know what makes us happy, and what we'd love to try out, and we may have a vague idea of how we'd go about it. But setting clear goals can be beneficial in several ways, above and beyond wishful thinking: here are a few.

How to Achieve Your Goals Consistently?

Effective goal setting requires consideration of the system that surrounds you. Too often, we set the right goals inside the wrong system. If you're fighting your system each day to make progress, then it's going to be hard to make consistent progress.

All kinds of hidden forces make our goals easier or harder to achieve. You need to align your environment with your ambitions if you wish to make progress in the long run. Let's discuss some practical strategies for doing just that.

How to Align Your Environment with Your Goals?

Although most of us have the freedom to make a wide range of choices at any given moment, we often make decisions based on the environment we find ourselves in. For example, if I wanted to do so, I could drink a beer as I write this guide. However, I am currently sitting at my desk with a glass of water next to me. There are no beers in sight. Although I possess the capability to get up, walk to my car, drive to the store, and buy a beer, I probably won't because I am surrounded by easier alternatives. In this case, taking a sip of water is the default decision, the easy decision.

Similarly, many of the decisions we make in our professional and personal lives are shaped by the options that surround us.

> ➢ If you sleep with your phone next to your bed, then checking social media and email as soon as you wake up is likely to be the default decision.

- ➤ If you walk into your living room and your couches and chairs all face the television, then watching television is likely to be the default decision.
- ➤ If you keep alcohol in your kitchen, then drinking consistently is more likely to be the default decision.

Of course, defaults can be positive as well.

- ➤ If you keep a dumbbell next to your desk at work, then pumping out some quick curls is more likely to be the default decision.
- ➤ If you keep a water bottle with you throughout the day, then drinking water rather than soda is more likely to be the default decision.
- ➤ If you place floss in a visible location (like next to your toothbrush), then flossing is more likely to be the default decision.

Scientists refer to the impact that environmental defaults can have on our decision-making as choice architecture. This has an important impact when it comes to achieving goals. Whether or not you achieve your goals in the long term has a lot to do with what types of influences surround you in the short term. It's very hard to stick with positive habits in a negative environment.

Here are a few strategies I have found useful when trying to design better default decisions in my life:

Simplicity. It is hard to focus on the signal when you're constantly surrounded by noise. It is more difficult to eat healthy when your kitchen is filled with junk food. It is more difficult to focus on reading a blog post when you have 10 tabs open in your browser. It is more difficult to accomplish your most important task when you fall into the myth of multitasking. When in doubt, eliminate options.

HOW TO SET GOALS

What is goal setting to you? When you set goals, are you used to seeing them disappear in the rearview mirror? We're willing to bet if you're reading this page, you've set a goal or two in your life. But did you see them through?

You're much more likely to put time and energy into something that excites you, so your goals must reflect that same level of momentum. Think of a goal as a dream with a deadline. Now all we have to do is create a_blueprint for achievement.

1. PERFORM A BRAINSTORMING SESSION.

Give yourself six minutes to brainstorm a list of anything you'd like to achieve, create, do, have, give and/or experience in the next 20 years. Write as many items down as fast as you can in this time. Use the rocking chair test to come up with ideas: Picture yourself in retirement, thinking back on your life from your rocking chair. What accomplishments will you be most proud of? What will you most regret? These are your most important answers to the question, "Why is goal setting important?"

2. Goal Design

The first step is to design our goals. When crafting goals, we need to remember the key premise of goal-setting theory — that they are intentions which guide our behaviour. They are "targets for mental action sequences"

Ideally, by design:

- ➢ Goals should be concrete endpoints. That is, we should be able to measure our success because they are clear and detailed;
- ➢ They should be approach-based. This means we should easily be able to focus on moving positively towards their accomplishment, rather than away from negative outcomes. ("Working toward" rather than "avoiding" something) and
- ➢ We should be able to break them down into sub-goals if necessary so that we can celebrate little successes along the way

Setting deadlines is crucial to goal setting. Go back through your list and write one, three, five, 10 or 20 years next to each goal to indicate how long it will take to achieve them. Some goals take a lifetime to achieve, but make sure you are pushing yourself toward both professional and personal growth. If you don't know how long a goal will take – like finding a healthy relationship – write down how long you would like it to take. Remember: "Goals are like magnets. They'll attract the things that make them come true."

This logical thinking process tool is an excellent way to maintain focus on your goal while considering the strategy you might use to achieve it. The very top of the tree is the end goal – your mission statement. On the next level are a maximum of five objectives that are critical to attaining your main goal.

Under the objectives are the necessary conditions required to achieve each one. A goal tree is like a map to success, over time each step is colour coded as it is completed, meaning that you can easily review your progress at a glance.

3. Be optimistic but realistic

If you set an unrealistic goal, it may well discourage you from continuing with your endeavours.

4. Evaluate your goals and reflect upon them

Feedback is superior to no feedback, and self-generated feedback is more powerful than externally generated feedback

After setting your goal, feedback is the best way to assess how well you are doing. Try setting up a schedule where you can 'check in' on your progress every week. Do you need to reassess and redefine your goal?

5. Believe in your abilities

Believe in your abilities, but know that it's OK if things aren't going to plan. Re-evaluating our progress and rethinking goals are all part of the process. Remember that any progress towards your goal is a good thing.

6. CONNECT YOUR GOALS TO YOUR PURPOSE.

Go over what you've written. Choose your top four one-year goals. These are goals that excite you because they are most connected to your purpose in life. Write a paragraph for each goal explaining why you will achieve this goal within the next 12 months. This isn't a to-do list. This is creating a vision for your life. When you have a powerful reason for "why," you'll more easily discover the "how."

7. CREATE SMART GOALS.

Now it's time to take those big goals and break them down into smaller SMART goals. Are your goals specific? Measurable? Achievable? Realistic? Do they have a specific timeframe? These are the components of a SMART goal. Breaking down your goals in this way sets a strong purpose and intention, making them more concrete and easier to achieve. You'll also be able to better track your progress and celebrate your successes – two keys to achieving goals we'll talk about next.

HOW TO ACHIEVE YOUR GOALS

Learning how to set goals is worthless if you don't learn how to achieve goals. Set yourself up for success by following these tips.

1. VISUALIZE YOUR GOALS

Where focus goes, energy flows, so it's critical to focus on your goals. Visualization is one powerful way to do this. When you visualize your goals daily as if you've already achieved them, you align your purpose and values with your actions. Everyone from star athletes to entrepreneurs uses visualization as well as practices like vision boards to help with goal setting. You can even tape images of your goals on the mirror in your bathroom or pin them to the wall next to your computer. If your goals involve adopting a healthy diet and losing weight, put them on the front of your refrigerator or a kitchen cabinet.

2. KEEP YOURSELF ACCOUNTABLE

Find a friend, family member or another person you trust and share your list of goals with them. You can also share the list with a mentor or life coach. Sharing your list will make you more accountable and give you a partner who will work with you through frustrations or roadblocks. The right partner can help you transform obstacles into opportunities and stay on track.

3. TRACK YOUR PROGRESS

Have a set schedule to review both short- and long-term goal setting. This helps you track progress as well as determine what activities are helping you and which are hindering you. It's important to know when you need to make alterations to your course. As Tony says, "Stay committed to your decisions but stay flexible in your approach." Don't lose sight of your ultimate goal, but remember that life is happening for you, not to you.

The following broad guidelines will help you to set effective, achievable goals:

- **State each goal as a positive statement** – Express your goals positively – "Execute this technique well" is a much better goal than "Don't make this stupid mistake."
- **Be precise** – Set precise goals, putting in dates, times and amounts so that you can measure achievement. If you do this, you'll know exactly when you have achieved the goal and can take complete satisfaction from having achieved it.
- **Set priorities** – When you have several goals, give each a priority. This helps you to avoid feeling overwhelmed by having too many goals and helps to direct your attention to the most important ones.
- **Write goals down** – This crystallizes them and gives them more force.
- **Keep operational goals small** – Keep the low-level goals that you're working towards small and

achievable. If a goal is too large, then it can seem that you are not making progress towards it. Keeping goals small and incremental gives more opportunities for reward.

➢ **Set performance goals, not outcome goals** – You should take care to set goals over which you have as much control as possible. It can be quite dispiriting to fail to achieve a personal goal for reasons beyond your control! In business, these reasons could be bad business environments or unexpected effects of government policy. In sports, they could include poor judging, bad weather, injury, or just plain bad luck. If you base your goals on personal performance, then you can keep control over the achievement of your goals, and draw satisfaction from them.

➢ **Set realistic goals** – It's important to set goals that you can achieve. All sorts of people (for example, employers, parents, media, or society) can set unrealistic goals for you. They will often do this in ignorance of your desires and ambitions. It's also possible to set goals that are too difficult because you might not appreciate either the obstacles in the way or understand quite how much skill you need to develop to achieve a particular level of performance.

Example Personal Goals

For his New Year's Resolution, Girish has decided to think about what he wants to do with his life.

His lifetime goals are as follows:

- ➤ **Career** – "To become sr manager in his company"
- ➤ **Physical** – "To run a gym."

Now that Girish has listed her lifetime goals, he then breaks down each one into smaller, more manageable goals.

Let's take a closer look at how he might break down his lifetime career goal – becoming managing editor of his magazine:

- ➤ **Five-year goal:** "Become an sr manager."
- ➤ **One-year goal:** "Volunteer for projects that the current Managing."
- ➤ **Six-month goal:** "Update with new technology and skills"
- ➤ **One-month goal:** "Talk to the current manager to determine what skills are needed to do the job."
- ➤ **One-week goal:** "Understand the process."

As you can see from this example, breaking big goals down into smaller, more manageable goals make it far easier to see how the goal will get accomplished.

Key Points

Goal setting is an important method for:

- ➤ Deciding what you want to achieve in your life.
- ➤ Separating what's important from what's irrelevant, or a distraction.
- ➤ Motivating yourself.
- ➤ Building your self-confidence, based on the achievement of goals.

Set your lifetime goals first. Then, set a five-year plan of smaller goals that you need to complete if you are to reach your lifetime plan. Keep the process going by regularly reviewing and updating your goals. And remember to take time to enjoy the satisfaction of achieving your goals when you do so.

If you don't already set goals, do so, starting now. As you make this technique part of your life, you'll find your career accelerating, and you'll wonder how you did without it!

CELEBRATE YOUR SUCCESSES

Goal setting doesn't have to be a boring set of tasks to check off. When you're planning your goals, including ways to celebrate your successes. If you're working toward financial freedom, set aside a budget for a nice dinner when you reach a certain goal. Celebrate relationship milestones. Got that promotion? Share it with the world and celebrate. It will help you stay focused – while also being present at the moment.

Why is goal setting important? Imagine yourself older and looking back. What's the pain of not achieving, and what is the pleasure of having achieved your goals? Effective goal setting helps you stay focused, keeps you accountable and is the single most important aspect of reaching your dreams.

Chapter – 11
You are unstoppable, Have Faith in you

There is something funny about a person's confidence. It can often be at a high or low level in just a matter of a short time. Faith in yourself is often important when you want to work on something. Believe in yourself and you will be unstoppable. You should maintain your self-belief all the time as you want the best results from what you do.

Have you ever been in a situation when you seriously don't believe in your capability?

That moment might be hard. When you feel unconfident about yourself, whatever things you do just don't seem right. You won't think that you will get a good result from your work. You are uncomfortable with the approaches that you use and you often just think about bad things.

That is often the main ingredient for a bad situation that may come. As we will see in the following description, it is something that you must avoid immediately. Believe in yourself and you will be unstoppable. Do otherwise and that will be not good for you.

The Continuous Cycle

When you don't have faith in what you can do, it leads you to think that you will do badly. That leads to a much bigger possibility of bad results from the work. That is something which you surely don't want, right?

When you have bad results, it can decrease your confidence further. You may think of them as evidence that you cannot do anything right. That lower confidence will lead to bigger possibilities for the next bad results. The cycle will keep going on and on if there isn't anything you do to stop it.

Certainly, you want to escape from this kind of bad cycle. Bad things can lead to bad things. Yet, the opposite is true also and it is the thing that we must strive ourselves for.

Our thoughts about ourselves are often self-fulfilling things. As the famous quote from Henry Ford says: "Whether you think you can or think you can't, you're right." The thinking about what we can do often manifests itself in our reality.

Our capability can certainly be improved and we should be able to learn from our experience. It is often a matter of knowing what are our mistakes and fine-tunes from there.

But, when we already think that we cannot and there is nothing that we can do, that is a distracting problem. You should always believe that you can do something if it is something important to you. As you do it with confidence, you may compensate for it with the things that you learn by doing.

Believe in yourself and you will be unstoppable. There are certain things that you can do to improve your self-confidence. Remembering past success or reading some motivation and self-improvement materials should be great. You may also set some milestones for your progress to success and accomplish it. Whatever you do, keep in mind that you can always do something for the best results. It is often a matter of maintaining faith in yourself that you can do such a thing.

You should believe in yourself and you will be unstoppable. Keep on moving forward and be confident in your capability. You should be able to unlock the ideal living situation for yourself much easier that way.

Always Do Your Best

Whatever work that you do, whether it is something that you think will produce small or big results for you, it is important to always do your best especially if it is something related to the success that you want to have. By always putting in the greatest effort that you can give, there will not be any regret in the future and you will not miss any good opportunity that might just show up if you just put in the optimum effort.

You might think that the things that you work on currently do not deserve your full attention. Being asked to occupy the company booth to attract the event visitor when you are one of the directors in the company? Going to inspect one of your smallest branches when you are the CEO? There might be some thinking that those jobs should be done by someone else and not you. Because of that thinking, when you have to do them, you will not give your best effort because you think the tasks are not for you to do and you should be doing something else more meaningful and suitable for you.

However, it is important that you always do your best in whatever you do. The booth might attract some important clients and you might discover something important for your company's business performance improvement when you go to that smallest branch. The thing here is you might never know what good things you can have from the work by giving it your hardest. The sure thing is that you will not have the chance to get them if your effort is half-hearted.

Taking the Lead Because You Always Do Your Best

Now, when you see someone who does his/her best at work, usually you will be inspired to give your highest effort too. You will feel shame for that person if you only give a half-hearted effort. Because of that, the outcome of the team will surely be better because everyone is inspired to give everything that they got.

Giving example by always doing your best is one of the greatest things that you can do when you lead a team because the others will see and will be motivated too to work optimally. They see that their leader tries his/her best and should be inspired to try to do so also in each of their respective functions.

So, try to set an example and inspire other team members to do the same. You cannot ask others to put in the effort when you do not do it yourself.

Even if you work alone, you can give inspiration to your future self by always doing your best. This maximum effort thing can become a great habit if you do it consistently and your future self can get used to it. Optimum work usually results in the best results that you can achieve and that sure is good for the realization of things that you want to aim for by doing the work.

The Good Things that Can Come

Always doing your best is also important in terms of the opportunities that can be opened. You might not know that your current work will give you the outcomes that take you much closer to your success. You may only know it after the work process. Therefore, do your optimum work every time and the opportunities will not have the chance to pass you by.

If you do things badly, then not only the doors are closed for you to get something important from the work. You will not learn something in the process as a result of your low motivation to do it. You might think that the things that you can learn from the work process are not important thus you neglect to understand them. However, the personal development that you should do can benefit from any positive things that you can learn. The work that you do must have something positive that you can take and this is the thing that you should focus on taking when you finish the work.

Who knows if the opportunity that might come to you in the future is related to the things that you can learn during the current work process? Always do your best and keep an open mind so you can process anything positive in the work that you do.

Always doing your best is something important and it will take time for you to get used to it if you have not made it a habit yet every day. Do whatever you must do and always try to do it well every day to get the best results, open the best opportunities, and learn the best lessons that you can get from that work process.

"You can have anything you want if you are willing to give up the belief that you can't have it."

- Dr Robert Anthony –

Do you believe that you can accomplish something big in life? When it comes to achievement, we sometimes belittle ourselves. We think we don't have enough capability to get to the top and enjoy achievements like the most successful people.

However, when we think about it, it is often a self-fulfilling prophecy. When we don't have faith in our capabilities, we won't start putting in the <u>work</u> needed to achieve <u>success</u>. That, in turn, means we won't succeed in life because we aren't even willing to take the first step needed. Logically, we won't get from A to B if we don't want to move ourselves to the destination.

"Whether you think you can or you can't, you're right." This quote from Henry Ford, one of the most successful entrepreneurs himself of his era, sums it up perfectly. If you already think you can't, most probably you won't do what it takes to succeed. On the other hand, if you think you can, it opens the door for you to realize big goals in life.

Therefore, it is important to have faith in yourself. It is so you can give yourself a chance to become the best version of yourself.

Believe in yourself and keep <u>putting in the effort consistently</u> towards the things you want in life. That is the basic principle of success that you should keep in mind.

It might be a long road ahead and it may be filled with struggles and problems. However, as long as you have faith in your capabilities and keep on moving forward, you should achieve success eventually

Self-Motivation

If you are already an adult, the life you walk in at the moment is the culmination result of all your choices and actions you made in the past. The lesson learned in life is that you cannot go away from the fact that you are the one who is the most responsible for your life condition, whether

it is a condition which you wanted or not. This is a self-motivation message for you.

The person who never takes responsibility for his/her bad condition in life is most likely to never have the self-motivation needed to change course on his/her road to success. What are the lessons learned in life by successful people?

We, as a human, seem to naturally have a bias regarding the lessons learned in life related to the condition of our present time. If the one which we go through right now is a good life, most of us will probably think that it is mostly the result of our work on the road to success. But if it is a bad one which we are having now, our self-motivation is inclined towards blaming other people or another external factor that affects our life miserably and so, in our version of lessons learned in life, it seems like the situation will be a lot better, that we will still be firmly on the road to success, if it is not just because of this person's doing or it is not because that factor happens on which we do not have any control of.

Well, guess what? We must take lessons learned in life about the responsibility the <u>bad condition </u>too and it is because the more we blame external factors as the main cause, the more it is that we never have the self-motivation to come out from that bad situation and get back on the road to success. It is unlikely that the condition can be turned for the better because we lack the self-motivation to change it, no lessons learned in life to change our situation, and no self-motivation to keep going on the road to success.

The Importance of Self-Motivation and Responsibility on the Road to Success

Let's take an example of a man who probably has it rather rough on his road to success. He has divorced the woman he loves so much and has little to no money in his bank account at the moment. Lessons learned in life from his take is that he blames his divorce on his wife because the wife is being in love with someone else during their marriage and he blames his state of no money on his employees who steer the company he founded into bankruptcy. He says that it is a result of bad executions from the business decisions which he made for the company.

I think this thinking is one of the worst lessons learned in life he can take from his journey on the road to success about his condition at the moment.

Why? Because by continuing to blame someone or something else for the bad condition in his finance and love condition at the moment, absolving himself of the blame in the process, will make him **less likely to take the right lessons in life and have the self-motivation that he can change the situation** with his action in the road to success.

There will be less likely self-motivation to try to find another woman to marry if he thinks that he is in trauma and that the lessons learned in life are that he cannot make a woman not have an affair with another guy and he will most probably lack the self-motivation to start a new business, going on again in his road to success, which will have its employees again because of the lessons learned in life about mistrust of another person working for him based on his reflection of previous business experience.

How about putting it in another way? If the lessons learned in life for him are different, he thinks his divorce is because, probably, *he* does not give enough time to his wife and his financial condition at the moment is because *he* does not give enough attention to evaluate what his employees have already done in terms of the execution from the business decisions he makes or he suspects that he does not give the best decision to be run by his employees, *he* can have the self-motivation to fix the situation mostly by himself by lessons learned in life from his experiences and get back to the road to success faster. He can try to allocate more time to spend with the next woman that he chooses to be with for the rest of his life and he can learn more about how to supervise his employees better or try to practice more in terms of leadership and management, while evaluating his decision making, and probably consulting to some expert or mentor about business decisions to make himself a firmer ground on his road to success. That is some self-motivation needed to change the bad condition.

The most important thing is that if he takes the lessons learned in life that it was himself who is the most responsible for the failures that happen to him, he can have the self-motivation to improve himself to be capable to change the failure condition to success shortly. If the lessons learned in life are the reason for their bad condition because of external factors that they cannot control, then he most probably lacks the self-motivation to be in better condition again because there is nothing that he believes he can do about it. Your self-motivation to progress on the road to success can have an important moment on how you react to this kind of situation.

Lessons Learned in Life About Personal Responsibility

So after you accept the responsibility for your failure, you are more likely to reflect on yourself and have enough self-motivation to try again so it can be a smoother ride on the road to success next time. That is the lessons learned in life which you should take about your bad experience.

This is, I believe, why a person's mindset should be that whatever happens to that person is a personal responsibility, whatever condition that person is in now is that person's responsibility. He/she can have the self-motivation and power to change it if that is the case. You should be strong enough to accept this as your lessons learned in life on your road to success.

Because "This failure is because of something that I cannot control" is just not a good enough belief for us to achieve the success that we want. Success is something which we, ourselves, must put a lot of effort in its direction to achieve it. Only by believing in ourselves on the ability to achieve it, accepting that sometimes we can have a mistake and fail, then choosing to put the effort in again based on lessons learned in life to make the best effort that the failure will not happen again in the future, go forward again on the road to success towards achieving it, then we can make sure that success is something that we deserve to have, that it is our right to get it because of our effort and accountability.

Thus, please don't be afraid to fail, and don't be afraid to take any responsibility for the situation on your road to success. The lessons learned in life should get yourself back up, believe that success is your own and your responsibility, and move forward again with the belief and your effort to achieve your success.

Chapter – 12
The Journey from Worrier to Warrior

Battlefield of Life

Life is a battle. You not only fight external battles with the world outside but also internal battles with your own destructive and evil qualities. The world in which you live is a battlefield. Your mind and body are also battlefields. It is where you fight physical and mental battles against your own evil, negative, or unlawful tendencies, qualities, desires, thoughts and attitudes. In the sacrifice of life, you serve both good and evil. Sometimes circumstances and sometimes your desires and expectations influence your actions and decisions.

Your life is shaped by which side you stay and against whom you fight. Every day when you step out of the bed, you enter the battlefield of the world. Every day, you have to choose between your constructive and destructive thoughts and desires, and between your compulsions and your ideals.

Therefore, the message of the Bhagavadgita is very relevant. Its symbolism can be applied to your daily life. Arjuna is your wakeful self. It symbolizes his confusion, sorrow, and suffering in the face of a crisis. Krishna, the wise teacher, is your wisdom. It is what restores your balance and confidence and puts sense in your thoughts and actions. Your senses are Sanjaya, the observer. Your selfishness is Dhritarashtra, the ego. Your selfless thoughts are Pandavas and their army, the forces of light. Your selfish thoughts are Kauravas and their army, the forces of darkness. Your whole mind-body complex is the battlefield - Kshetra.

Will you be a warrior or a worrier?

We live in times of rapid change and complexity, which evoke feelings of uncertainty. While it is normal to have worries in life; at the most trying of times, worrying can manifest and become a chronic problem for some.

Feeling trapped in a vicious cycle of worrying can make people feel emotionally stressed and physically drawn, leading to disruptive conditions like sleep problems, inability to carry out daily routines, depression, and negative feelings of withdrawal from life.

Feeling good about ourselves is not a luxury, it is our life-long essential for good mental and physical health – We need to worry less and start living!

How to be a worrier:

Be a worrier by projecting pessimism onto the future, mistakenly believing that whatever is going wrong now will be around forever.

Be a worrier by battening down the hatches, sitting tight, and waiting for this all to blow over. Worry so much about doing the wrong thing that instead you do nothing. Worry that a brighter future doesn't lie ahead and accept that things are awful and probably always will be.

Worry externally about the people you speak to. Lose all sense of worth, undersell or undervalue what you do. Lower your standards and convince yourself that you're lucky to have anything. Heavily discount. Aim to break even. Let your worry lead to a mindset of scarcity, where you are convinced there will never be enough to go around.

Hark back to the good old days and wish they were back. Keep your fingers crossed for "normal". Daydream about how good things used to be. Fear they won't be that good again. Worry that this all lies on your shoulders and that your people are counting on you. Feel the weight of that pressure. Believe they are helpless without you and worry even more. Overestimate the competition and underestimate your ability. Be led by imposter syndrome. Speculate based on dread.

Your thoughts shape your actions and your mindset. If you find yourself caught in worry-based unhelpful thought patterns, snap out of them before they shape your present moment and your future existence.

How to be a warrior:

Be a warrior by waking up with the undoubtable belief that you are wholly equipped to get through whatever is thrown at you. Nod confidently to yourself. Find the game in overcoming challenges and daring them to break you. Don't be surprised when they don't. Tell yourself that this is a test. Act accordingly.

Sleep soundly each night knowing that tomorrow is when you'll put your best thinking into action. Thrive at the chance to start again. Recognise that being knocked back a few steps is the chance to rebuild stronger. Do it the same, but better. Anti-fragile. Re-find the excitement and the passion.

Leave no stone unturned. Question everything. Why didn't that work? How can I improve? Find how you can advance. Continue with the dead certs and the remarkable ideas and park everything else. Rally your troops and unite them for the cause. Inspire them to up their games. Carry no one. Strengthen your weakest links and cut your losses.

Forget about the news. Forget about opinion and judgment. What you know for sure is that 80% of this is within your control, and the other 20% is anyone's guess. Focus on the 80%. Be open to learning, not closed to improvement. Take advice only from those you would accept criticism.

One day, you'll look back at the week you're about to have and assess what you did. In this decision lies the chance to make it the week that everything changed. Make it the week where a switch was flicked, and you stepped up your game. Look back on it as being the best thing that ever happened to you. Marvel at how much you were capable of. Choose to be a warrior, not a worrier.

'Be a Warrior, not a Worrier'

It is so easy to let things worry us, way more than they should. Sometimes we are not even sure what we are worrying about. We tend to make up stories and scenarios in our head of 'what if', 'how will I?', and Could it be that...?' when in reality, we would have no visibility of what will happen. This is what makes us worriers.

What if we try to shift our mindset from being a worrier to being a warrior? What if we stop worrying about what could happen, and instead use our energy to transform ourselves into warriors to be ready for whatever happens? We would then be able to put our worries aside because we would be ready for whatever life decides to throw at us.

Let's all try to jumble up our vowels and turn from worries into warriors.

Finding Light in the Darkness

When we can no longer change a situation, we are challenged to change ourselves," said Victor Frankly. How true that is.

But the power to change does not solely exist in times when we are pushed up against a wall or at the end of our rope — it happens every day. As we grow our consciousness to experience reality from a more spiritual vantage point, we realize that the good, the bad, the ups, the downs, and each singular challenge we face exist so that we can progress into something more than we are today. We are tested in life because it is through those tests that we reveal who we are — to „show a dn what we're made of," as they say.

When facing our obstacles, we think: How can I escape this situation? How can I avoid this? How can I find a way NOT to deal with this? Either this or we enter into that dark alleyway of doubting the existence of the light in our lives at all. Maybe we begin to question the validity of our path, choices, and spirituality. We forget all the miracles that we have already seen.

But in every day (and not so every day) struggles there sits an opportunity for growth. You can find empowerment in the open window when all doors become closed; to find that place inside where we have the strength and certainty to accept our challenges, knowing there is always a way, there is always a path towards overcoming, even if it does not look like what we would picture as a perfect solution.

Sometimes the first step is just as simple as taking the empowered mental stance of, „OKAY, here is the challenge before me. I know the light is here despite the darkness I am experiencing. How can I face this in a positive way?"

Spirituality isn't something that just happens. As there is breath in our lungs, there is always some sort of trial by fire. It is in the acceptance, the struggle, the certainty and the overcoming, that we reveal and grow our inner power.

No matter the obstacle we are facing, the spiritual challenge remains the same—that we "come with our days," living each and every moment to find the light that exists in the darkness. The first step, of course, is the simple knowledge that the light is there.

The Story of Nick Vujicic

The journey from worrier to warrior

Creating a Life Without Limbs

This is Why You Need to Have a Lion Like an Attitude and Belief

Nick Vujicic was born with an extremely rare disability. Despite this, he overcomes many obstacles and becomes a leader to millions of people worldwide.

Nick Vujicic proved to the world, That it's the power of attitude and belief that shape your life.

Maybe you are familiar with Nick Vujicic, but if you are not, then you should be! Because his inspirational life story will make you speechless.

Why attitude and belief are everything?

If there is something that can change your life, it is your attitude and belief about yourself.

If you are not sure then Just look at this great man Nick Vujicic who has no legs, and no arms but he can still swim. He can play football and hockey and he can skydive.

He is an author and motivational speaker, He has written some very famous books like Unstoppable, Life without Limits, and Life Without Limbs.

How the heck is this possible in this world?

He has so many reasons to find excuses but no! He won't, Instead, he is there to inspire the whole world, Me and you.

Nick Vujicic wants to show to the world, That I might be disabled bodily but I won't stay back, I will never give up on my dreams, And I will do the impossible.

The only reason he is doing the impossible is his attitude and belief, He knows things are difficult, but he makes sure that he is tougher than situations.

No one can stop a man with the right mental attitude from achieving his goals.

Nothing on the earth can help a man with the wrong attitude. – Thomas Jefferson

Nick Vujicic's early life struggles

Nick Vujicic Was born in 1984 in Australia, He was born abnormal, A child with no legs and arms.

He didn't live a very good life at an early age, Because of his looks and body shape he was bullied, Others made fun of him and laughed at him.

He was so worried and so depressed thinking that I'm done, with the Bullying at school, All the teasing. Do my mom and dad ever know If I am going to get married. I Don't know if I am ever going to be independent, If I don't have a purpose then what's the point, if my pains not going to change?

At this point, He was hopeless, He thought this is the end and he wanted to **commit suicide.**

Why me? I am sure you have asked this question yourself a lot of times, and so did Nick Vujicic.

I asked my parents why this happened, but they dint' have the answer, I asked my doctor but he also didn't know it.

He had a lot of questions, that needed to be answered, but who would do it for him? Who would answer his words? All of his brothers were fine but why only him?

This thought kept him thinking, He was not able to live a normal life, he was depressed, and hopelessness was killing him from the inside.

He was 10 when he thought to finish his life and Eliminate all these pains. But something kept him there, and he was able to hold on.

Nick Vujicic's belief kept him strong

My doctor told me that you are not going to be able to walk, but today I am walking.

Nick Vujicic's Doctor told him, that he can't walk, but he didn't think of what his doctor said and did what he wanted to do.

Today he is not only walking but also, he can play. He plays soccer, and hockey, and Even he can swim.

He would always think about what's unique about him, what's different, and good about him. So he would look into the mirror and say, Nick, you have pretty eyes.

Even in this type of body, he would find at least something good about him, which would keep him motivated to live a better life.

Now he is a motivational speaker and author, his voice is spread all over the world. He has inspired millions of people.

No hands no legs no worries- But He doesn't even consider himself disabled

When an interviewer asked him, you have no arms and legs, he replied, No arms no legs no worries. He says disability is what stops you from doing something.

That's the power of attitude and belief, He doesn't even consider himself disabled, He believes that everyone is going through something bad in life, And the only reason he is highlighted is that his pain is visible.

This is so true, we all are having problems in our lives, and the only thing that keeps us holding on is our beliefs and attitude.

If you have the right kind of attitude, you will see the obstacles as opportunities.

The turning point of Nick's life

When Nick was 17, His mother gave him a newspaper, in which he read an article about a disabled man, who was successful.

This article changed his life, He realized the power of attitude and belief. He knew that if he believes in himself and keeps a positive attitude, the World will be at his feet.

From there he didn't look back and tried whatever he could to achieve his dreams. He wanted to inspire everyone, He wanted to give a message to all disabled people, That it's not the end.

His dream came true in 2005 When he built his first non-profit Organization, Life Without Limbs. The purpose of this company was to give a better life to disabled people.

In 2007 he found another company, called **Attitude is Altitude**, where he gives motivational speeches.

What do we learn from Nick Vujicic?

The power of attitude

There is one thing Nick's life teaches us is, your attitude determines your altitude.

If your attitude towards your life is positive, you can do anything, limits are just myths. They don't exist in reality, It's you who creates limits for yourself.

Dr Myles Munroe gave a very good example of why attitude is everything.

The lion is not the tallest of the animals. It is not the smartest of animals, and it is the most powerful animal. But still, it's the king of the jungle.

The elephant is smarter, Taller, and more powerful than The lion, but what happens when the elephant sees the Lion? There is one word that comes into its mind **Eater.**

It's not the size or intelligence that decides what you will do. If your attitude is like a Lion, you can do anything. The moment you decide, I will do whatever it takes, nothing can stop you.

It's the only difference between successful and broke people. Successful people have a positive attitude, they take chances, and they know each problem is an opportunity.

Opportunity to learn more, to get more, and to be more. They always ask what to do better, instead of blaming people or situations, and this is what makes them different from ordinary people.

So that's it, that was the story of Nick Vujicic to inspire you, and to show you the power of attitude and belief.

Feeling lost in life?

Not until we are lost do we begin to understand ourselves." -Henry David Thoreau.

You are not alone mate. We all feel lost sometimes. Just because people don't seem this way on the outside, doesn't mean they don't feel these emotions inside. It's hard when you're surrounded by people your age whom all seem like they have their life together, but in reality, they are just really good at faking it. Even the people who are successful now once felt lost in life.

Even if you feel lost in life now, do not give up. Whether you had a terrible childhood or you've suffered from some difficult experiences in life, you should be thankful for it. Why? Because the struggle you are in today is developing the strength you need for tomorrow.

As long as you are alive, you still have a chance.

"The most successful people are the ones who never give up..."

Sometimes the hardest moments in your life are guiding you in the right direction. Sometimes bad things have to happen to make space for something great. Let me say this one time, you can be full of love and light and still have a bad day. Let life happen, and have faith in you that god has better plans for you.

First, admit that you are unhappy, then admit why, then understand how you should get back up, and then you need to let go of the things which are pulling you down. Allow yourself a moment. Breath in the moment deeply then the healing process will begin

When challenges come your way, identify growth opportunities, how can flip the seemingly negative into something that can help you rise? While life isn't always perfect and fair, and not all days are sunshine, the bad stuff can help us to create more of the great stuff.

It's okay to talk about the things you feel, about your depression, your anxiety and your stress and all the things you worry about, it's okay to struggle with these things to how to deal with them. to not know where to begin or how to deal with it or how to heal, it's all okay my friend but don't keep everything inside you. Talk about how you feel and what you feel, be honest and be open about it. it's okay to break down in tears, this is how you change, and this is how you will heal, by talking about it and by letting the people who care about you to know, what it is you holding so far. Don't bottle up inside in your heart, don't bury it and let it out and let the sunlight in like this your journey begins, yeah like this properly you grow.

Friendly reminder my friend! Whatever it is that is causing you pain and all of this stress. All of this anxiety, worries, and depression will pass, have faith in yourself and you will survive like a monster and move on with experiences, as you always have a bad day, and tomorrow is a new one. Embrace the beauty of positivity and stay strong. No one breaks you, and you think you are broken inside but you are not. In the same way, you think you are lost but you are just discovering who you are.

On a serious note, I am proud of you mate! After everything you have been through, still you have managed to stay strong and heart open. And still, you have managed to smile. despite all the negative people put you through this. I'm proud of you that you are still here reading my words. remember you are making the best of things, I know you are alone, you are a true warrior look at you how far you have come. And alone is something to be proud of and inspired from. My mate I know you will be great at whatever it is you do and I can't wait to see what the future unfolds for you. I know you will make an impact trust me everything will work out in the end.

You know what my friend?

> It's okay to feel alone.

> It's okay to feel you are lost in the ocean.

> It's okay to feel empty and broken.

For everything lonely finds its company. Everything lost is meant to be found, everything empty is meant to get filled, and eventually, broken parts will be fixed.

Let's see will think like this my mate, think about all the terrible times you have lived through, just think about how they were and how it's all passed. You are a warrior on the battlefield, you have to go through hell to find heaven, likewise, you must break to find yourself whole again.

Buddy! you are a brave and strong person because life gives you every reason to give up and you still, rise, you shine and you pick yourself up and move forward with a wide smile. That's how you make the world better.

Water your bad days with love and patience, and watch as flowers grow from them tomorrow. In this era people do spend an entire day looking at their mobiles and laptop screens they are just attached to the reality that they don't exist. You have to keep those devices aside and Think about what you want, not what you don't want, guard your thoughts carefully, because they create your experiences. Sometimes you have to pause to appreciate yourself and how you have come. Remember self-appreciation is also a major key to kick start your inner energy

It's time for you to start taking the necessary steps and actions to become the version of yourself that you can't stop dreaming about. You know many peoples to be a burden on your goals, they come and feed all the negative thoughts in your head, if your voice in your head is mean to you, remember that someone manipulated that voice and installed it in you. Kill that fake voice and you must find yours. You know the ocean can't sink a ship unless it gets inside the ship, negativity can't sink you unless it gets inside you.

Printed in the USA
CPSIA information can be obtained
at www.ICGtesting.com
LVHW011613241023
761969LV00010B/81

9 789357 416726